Leaders of the Colonial Era

Peter
Stuyvesant

Leaders of the Colonial Era

Lord Baltimore

Benjamin Banneker

William Bradford

Benjamin Franklin

Anne Hutchinson

Cotton Mather

William Penn

John Smith

Miles Standish

Peter Stuyvesant

Leaders of the Colonial Era

Peter
Stuyvesant

Matt W. Cody

CHELSEA HOUSE
PUBLISHERS
An imprint of Infobase Publishing

To my mother, for sharing a love of history.

Chelsea House
An imprint of Infobase Publishing
132 West 31st Street
New York, NY 10001

Library of Congress Cataloging-in-Publication Data
Cody, Matthew W., 1974-
 Peter Stuyvesant / Matthew W. Cody.
    p. cm. — (Leaders of the colonial era)
 Includes bibliographical references and index.
 ISBN 978-1-60413-740-8 (hardcover)
 1. Stuyvesant, Peter, 1592-1672—Juvenile literature. 2. Governors—New York (State)—Biography—Juvenile literature. 3. New York (State)—History—Colonial period, ca. 1600-1775—Biography—Juvenile literature. 4. New Netherland—Biography—Juvenile literature. 5. New Amsterdam—Biography—Juvenile literature. I. Title. II. Series.
 F122.1.S78C63 2010
 974.7'102092—dc22
 [B]   2010010714

You can find Chelsea House on the World Wide Web at
http://www.chelseahouse.com

Text design by Kerry Casey
Cover design by Keith Trego
Composition by EJB Publishing Services
Cover printed by Bang Printing, Brainerd, Minn.
Book printed and bound by Bang Printing, Brainerd, Minn.
Date printed: November 2010
Printed in the United States of America

10 9 8 7 6 5 4 3 2 1

This book is printed on acid-free paper.

All links and Web addresses were checked and verified to be correct at the time of publication. Because of the dynamic nature of the Web, some addresses and links may have changed since publication and may no longer be valid.

Contents

1

The Future Leader of New Netherland

The year was 1644, and an ambitious young man was standing on board a ship in the middle of the Caribbean Sea. Bullets were whizzing all around him. He was caught in the middle of a ferocious battle between his countrymen, the Dutch, and their great rivals, the Spanish. At stake was nothing less than ownership of a crucial territorial possession. His employer, the Dutch West India Company, had told him to hold the island of St. Martin at any cost. St. Martin was rich in salt, a prized commodity at the time. For years, the Dutch and the Spanish had been warring over control of world trade routes, and now the new director of the Caribbean colonies was ready to make his move. After disembarking his ship with hundreds of soldiers at his command, the Spanish began a fierce attack. The young man was

Peter Stuyvesant was the leader of New Netherland, the colony that became New York.

hit in the right leg by a gunshot, and he fell to the ground. He was seriously wounded. His leg would have to be amputated below the knee.

The battle may have cost Peter Stuyvesant his leg, but it earned him a reputation for being a gritty soldier, a bold risk-taker, and a fearless leader. It was these qualities that prompted the Dutch West India Company to send Stuyvesant to its fledgling North American colony. Peter Stuyvesant was to become the leader of New Netherland.

A FUTURE METROPOLIS

The colony that Peter Stuyvesant took the helm of in 1647 was the ancestor of New York City. Most people know that New York State was one of the original thirteen English colonies and that New York City was once a former capital of the United States. However, there was a group of people that settled on the island of Manhattan before the English: the Dutch. Their settlement was called New Netherland. It included present-day New York City as well as parts of New Jersey, Connecticut, Pennsylvania, and Delaware. The settlement went as far north as Albany and far enough south to include all five modern-day boroughs of New York City.

A visit to New York City today reveals a vibrant, busy city of more than 8 million people tightly packed into an area of about 300 square miles. The city's inhabitants speak over 40 languages, practice many different religions, and hail from every country in the world. This great multicultural melting pot had its origin with New Netherland and its Dutch colonists. New Netherland was a society of many different peoples, religions, customs, and tastes. The story of how New Netherland became the diverse, cosmopolitan metropolis of New York City begins with the European explorers of the sixteenth century.

2

Exploring
the New World

The era of great European exploration began around 1500, but the story actually goes back a few hundred years before that. European merchants had been trading silk and spices with people in Asia since the 1200s. The route to Asia was traveled by some combination of land and sea. If one traveled by land, it was usually along the Silk Route, which connected China and western Asia. Traveling by land could be very dangerous, however. Local people often mistook foreign travelers for invaders. If the journey was made by sea, there were a number of possible routes, including sailing around the Cape of Good Hope at the southern tip of Africa. This, too, was difficult—not to mention time-consuming and expensive—despite the invention of the magnetic compass and other navigational tools. The high cost of making these journeys drove up the prices of goods that the Europeans desired. Merchants were tired of paying high prices for East Indian spices, for example, which were used to flavor food and preserve it. They simply needed to find another way—a less expensive more direct way—to Asia.

There were, however, other incentives for exploring the West. First, many countries had a great thirst for land and power. The more land a country owned, the more trade routes it controlled and the more powerful it became. A second reason had to do with the growing populations in Europe. New farmland was needed to grow enough crops to feed everyone. A third reason had to do with the expansion of Christianity. Christian nations during this time wanted to grow their sphere of influence by converting new peoples to Christianity.

MARCO POLO

Marco Polo is an example of a European merchant who traveled by land and sea to Asia in search of riches. Polo was born in Venice, Italy, around the year 1254. His father and uncle were explorers and traders and had become very rich from their work. On one of their voyages, they had an audience with Kublai Khan, the Mongolian emperor. After befriending the great leader, they were given messages from Kublai to take back to the pope. In 1271, young Marco accompanied them on a return trip by land to Asia. By 1275, they had arrived at the emperor's palace, and they stayed in Mongolia for 17 years. During these years, Marco Polo traveled all over lands that are today China and Mongolia. In 1290, the Polos set sail on a return trip to Venice. When they arrived home, they were greeted by astonished friends and family who believed they all had died years earlier.

THE NORTHWEST PASSAGE

In the late fifteenth century, European merchants and traders began their exploration of the West, hoping to find a direct route to Asia. The Italian explorer Christopher Columbus was hired by Spain to find a western path to the East Indies. He instead landed in what is today the Bahamas in the Caribbean Sea, discovering a "New World" for Spain and all of western Europe. After Columbus landed in the south, naturally it was thought that the path to Asia must be to the north and west. The search for this fabled "Northwest Passage" to Asia motivated European explorers for centuries. However, it was the success of Spanish and Portuguese explorers in the early sixteenth century that truly lit a fire under the ambitions of the other European navigators. Spanish explorers Francisco Pizarro and Hernán Cortés became extremely wealthy with their discoveries of silver in Peru and gold in Mexico, respectively.

England made the first transatlantic attempt when it sent an Italian explorer, Giovanni Caboto (known to history by his Anglicized name, John Cabot), across the Atlantic Ocean in 1497 to what is today Newfoundland. The Italian navigator Giovanni da Verrazano sailed for France in 1524, and he accomplished the first European exploration of the North American Atlantic coast, including New York Harbor and the Hudson River. The French explorer Jacques Cartier sailed down the St. Lawrence River in 1534, and Frenchman Samuel de Champlain discovered Quebec in 1608. After a number of these explorations were completed, it became clear that the northern lands of the New World were not Asia and did not have the gold and silver treasure of the south. What they did have, however, were riches of their own: plentiful natural resources such as animal furs and farmland along the Atlantic Coast that could grow corn, wheat, tobacco, and cotton.

Like the Spanish, French, English, and Portuguese, the Dutch were active in Asian trade. Eventually, they would explore the New

Christopher Columbus landed in the New World while trying to find a western path to the East Indies for Spain. This "discovery" prompted European powers to send exploration parties and people to colonize the area.

World, too. By the late sixteenth century, the Dutch were challenging Portugal's dominance of eastern sea routes to Asia and were anxious to find the rumored shortcut to the West.

HENRY HUDSON

The story of Dutch exploration of the New World begins, ironically, with an Englishman named Henry Hudson. Hudson was by all accounts very intelligent, ambitious, moody, and stubborn. By the time he had finished his travels, he had attempted to find the

Northwest Passage four separate times. Hudson lived in London, which was just a small market town at the beginning of the seventeenth century. Houses and shops were made of wood, and they lined narrow streets. Hudson's patron was a company called the Muscovy Company. It was formed, not surprisingly, by a group of merchants and wealthy men who saw a great business opportunity in the unknown lands across the Atlantic. They also saw a way to jump-start England's role as a player on the world stage. Up to this point, England existed in the shadow of Spain and Portugal. Spain and Portugal controlled the southern routes across the Atlantic. Furthermore, unlike those countries, England did not have a distinguished history of sea voyages, other than John Cabot's journey in 1497.

Accelerating the merchants' cause were the discoveries of another Englishman, a young man named John Dee. Dee obtained maps and globes when he was a student in Belgium and brought them back to London. These maps (including the Mercator projection that is still used today in school classrooms) were the first to show some detail of the area around the Arctic Circle. Among the details were passages and straits that appeared to show a northwest route across the Atlantic. The English merchants were tremendously excited. They pooled their money to form the Muscovy Company and armed their paid explorers with these maps, now certain in their ability to reach Asia via the Arctic Sea.

The first voyages of the Muscovy Company were unsuccessful in terms of finding the Northwest Passage. The ships actually sailed to the northeast and landed in Russia. However, this was a happy accident, for there were plenty of people in Russia ready to buy warm English wool for the brutal Russian winters. It was a boon for English wool makers and merchants. Years later, the wool trade with Russia would decline, and England's efforts to reach Asia via the Northwest Passage began anew.

HUDSON'S EARLY VOYAGES

Henry Hudson was already in his forties—a relatively old age—when he was approached by the Muscovy Company to work as an explorer for them. Despite being married with three sons, Hudson agreed. He would make four attempts in finding the Northwest Passage: three times for England and once for the Dutch. His first voyage in 1607 was a total disaster. In what seems like an unbelievable idea today, Hudson tried to go due north up over the top of the globe. Needless to say, he ran into massive chunks of ice, and because he was sailing in a wooden boat, this route was very dangerous. Further, the 12 men on his crew were living only on seal and bear meat (and often rotten bear meat at that) and were not in the mood to undertake such a futile mission. The attempt was a failure. Not dissuaded, Hudson sailed again the following year. In his second voyage, Hudson tried a northeasterly route, traveling the same path the earlier Muscovy explorers had attempted. In the middle of this voyage, Hudson apparently realized there was no hope going in this direction, and he changed course. Repositioned toward the northwest, his crew of 14 revolted, and Hudson was forced to return to London. When he approached the Muscovy Company about a third attempt, they refused to pay. Hudson felt dejected, and contemplated his next move. Little did he know he would be invited to try again by an entirely different country.

THE DUTCH EAST INDIA COMPANY

In 1602, the Dutch formed the Dutch East India Company, a trading company that paid navigators to sail to Asia via eastern routes. It was large, powerful, and well funded by the rich trade business that the Dutch were beginning to dominate. The Muscovy Company looked like a small shop compared to the Dutch East India Company. By 1609, the East India Company had its eye on the recently

Henry Hudson's ship, the *Half Moon*, meets Native Americans in the highlands of the Hudson River in 1609.

unemployed Hudson, hoping to expand its business to the West by finding a passage to Asia. It was in competition with the English (who now regretted their decision to let Hudson go) and the French, both of whom were trying to halt the growing power of the Dutch. If the Dutch were to find a shorter, more northern route to Asia, they would control world commerce.

The East India Company convinced Hudson to sign a contract, and his first voyage for the Dutch (and third overall) was aboard the ship *Halve Maen* ("Half Moon"). He departed in the spring of 1609. Interestingly, his Dutch employers urged him to try to find a northeastern route (as he had attempted before for England) rather than a northwestern route, as Hudson wished to do. The stubborn captain took matters into his own hands, changing course during his trip. He would sail to the northwest. Hudson was fortunate to have the notes of John Smith, the Englishman who had reached North America in 1607 and had set up the first permanent European settlement in Virginia. Smith's diagrams said that the best route was actually to the southwest, and after a number of weeks, Hudson found the entrance to Chesapeake Bay, where Smith had established his Jamestown Colony. Rather than paying them a visit (Hudson was sailing under the Dutch flag, after all, and the Dutch and English were bitter rivals), he turned north to the Delaware River, and then farther north into New York Harbor.

THE ISLAND OF *MANNA-HATA*

What Hudson sighted when he sailed into New York Harbor (as it would eventually be named) that day must have impressed him. He saw an island covered in trees and populated with natives. The native peoples living in North America were descended from people who are thought to have crossed the land bridge from Siberia to Alaska during the last ice age, which occurred some 11,500 years ago. Eventually migrating to nearly every corner of two continents, they were called "Indians" because, when Christopher Columbus saw them, he thought (and hoped) he had landed in the East Indies, in Asia. The tribes that lived around New Netherland included the Mahican, Mohawk, Lenape, Montauk, Manates, and Housatonic.

Hudson and his crew spied some Indians from the deck of the *Half Moon*. The people they saw were the Lenape (which means "real men"), also known as the Lenni Lenape ("we, the people"). Europeans would call them the "Delaware." The Lenape were hunters and fishermen and spoke the Algonquian language. They saw Hudson's ship (which they called a "house") and approached the crew peacefully. A descendant of an American Indian who was purportedly present at the meeting tells of a presentation of gifts including food, such as oysters, beans, and currants, and tools like knives and hatchets. Hudson and his crew continued to explore the area, gazing upon land that would someday be known as Brooklyn and New Jersey. They encountered more natives, but this time there was violence. As the author Russell Shorto notes, "It's ironic that immediately upon entering the watery perimeter of what would become New York City, these two things take place: trade and violence." (Shorto is referring to New York City's modern reputation for being both the center of world commerce and a city that struggles with crime.)

Led by Hudson, the *Half Moon* continued north, sailing up a river that would one day be named for him. Farther upriver, they came across yet more Indians, who offered beaver and otter furs to their European visitors in exchange for hatchets, knives, and beads. A fur trade was already under way to the north in present-day Canada between the French and other Indian groups. Furs, and specifically beaver furs, would come to be greatly desired by the Europeans, who used them to make coats and hats. Much of the trade with the New World over the next two centuries would be driven by the fur trade.

The river Hudson was on was called the *Manna-hata* by the Munsey, a subgroup of the native Lenape. The word most likely means "hilly island," "small island," or just "island." Eventually, the name would be transformed into "Manhattes" and then "Manhattan," and assigned to the island that lay alongside the river. Hudson quickly realized that this river was not going to lead them to Asia (the water was too shallow and the river too narrow) and decided to go home. Hudson set sail for Amsterdam but stopped in England first. While there, word of his discoveries got out, and the English decided they wanted him back. Hudson's fourth and final voyage would be for England.

HUDSON'S FINAL ATTEMPT

In his last attempt to find the Northwest Passage to Asia, Hudson finally decided to sail to the northwest. Trying to cut through the frozen waters north of Canada (eventually named Hudson Bay and Hudson Strait), his cold, sick, and starving crew ultimately turned on him. They put Hudson, his son, and other sick crew members on a boat and set it adrift in the freezing, barren sea. It is unknown where exactly Hudson froze to death, but it is thought to be somewhere in the southern part of the bay named for him.

Hudson's crew returned to London, and word spread to Amsterdam that Hudson had succeeded not in discovering a western route to Asia but perhaps something even better—a new, undiscovered land of furs. The Dutch, ever the entrepreneurs, got to work planning their next attempt to cross the Atlantic and lay claim to the new lands discovered by Henry Hudson.

3

The Birth
of New Netherland

In the seventeenth century, the Dutch found themselves in the midst of a Golden Age. They were leaders in many areas, including economics, education, art, and science. New Netherland developed as a direct result of the spirit of their accomplishments. The personality, religion, culture, and ambition of the Dutch people shaped their New World colony.

INDEPENDENCE FROM SPAIN

The nation that the Dutch inhabit today is called the Netherlands, but it was not always called that. The Dutch participated in a long, violent war with Spain from 1568 to 1648 called the Eighty Years' War. Spain was a Catholic country then (as it is today), and it controlled all of the lands of the so-called Low Countries (today, the Netherlands, Belgium, and Luxembourg). The king of Spain not only taxed the people living in the Low Countries, he also persecuted them because they were Protestant. In 1579, seven northern provinces, or states, revolted against Spain and united to form the Dutch Republic (also called the Republic of the Seven United Netherlands or the United Provinces). The southern provinces of the Low Countries continued to be controlled by Spain (and later Austria and France) until they eventually broke away to form the countries of Belgium and Luxembourg. These southern provinces were populated with the Flemish (or Flemings), who spoke Dutch, and the Walloons, who spoke French.

The most important province of the Dutch Republic was Holland, of which Amsterdam was the capital city. Holland, along with the six other provinces of Utrecht, Gelderland, Overijssel, Zeeland, Friesland, and Groningen, joined together to form a republican government. Each province had its own government, but there was a central government called the States-General that oversaw and unified them. The States-General was located in the city of The Hague.

CALVINISM

The Dutch were members of the Dutch Reformed Church, which was a branch of Protestantism based on the ideas of Calvinism. John Calvin was one of the early pioneers of Protestantism, along with Martin Luther, whose writings set off the Protestant Reformation in 1517. Among Calvin's beliefs was the idea that an individual could become closer to God by studying the Bible and finding meaning in it for him- or herself. This challenged the Catholic idea that only the pope and the hierarchy of Catholic leadership had the ultimate authority to spread God's word and interpret its meaning. Calvinism was also marked by a certain simplicity; for example, Calvin preferred a simple cross to the more dramatic Catholic images of Christ's suffering. Conflict between

Protestants and Catholics accounted for many of the wars in Europe for hundreds of years; indeed, the northern Dutch provinces' war of independence from Spain had its roots in Calvinist-Catholic tensions.

DUTCH SOCIETY

Dutch society was thriving economically, culturally, and intellectually in the early seventeenth century. The Dutch led the way in many fields, such as fine art (the great painters Rembrandt and Vermeer were from this era), economics (the Dutch were master shipbuilders, and that industry drove their dominance in world trade), science (Dutch scientists invented the microscope during this period), and education (the Dutch Republic was home to many of the world's greatest universities). As evidence of their intellectual strength, almost half the books published in the seventeenth century were printed and published in the Dutch Republic.

The Dutch prided themselves on being hardworking and believed that individuals could get ahead in society if they worked hard, a rather new concept for the time. They dressed less formally than, say, the English did and never put on airs. They lived in relatively simple houses, too. In fact, the idea of a "home" originates with the Dutch. In this period, many characteristics of our modern lifestyle began to emerge, such as homes having downstairs rooms for entertaining and upstairs rooms for private quarters. The Dutch were warm and affectionate with their children, which was also unusual for the times. Some religious groups in England, such as the Puritans, were very strict and aloof with their children.

RELIGIOUS TOLERANCE

The Dutch also had a reputation for tolerance of different people and ideas. Their society was driven by industry and commerce, and so they were usually willing to look the other way when welcoming different kinds of people into their country. Significantly, the Dutch were tolerant of different religions. Many Dutch cities of the era were populated with people from other countries, such as the Walloons and Flemings from the Low Countries, who had fled religious persecution.

If some of this sounds vaguely American, it's true. The Founding Fathers admired the Dutch for their lifestyle and ideals, especially those of individual responsibility, hard work, family life, and personal liberty. These are only some of the ways the Dutch would leave their stamp on America.

THE DUTCH WEST INDIA COMPANY

In 1621, the Dutch West India Company was formed. It was a companion to the East India Company, and it had exclusive rights to settle the Dutch possessions in the New World. The company intended to colonize the new lands, exploit the fur trade, and wage war on Spain and its New World and African colonies; in essence, it was a corporation with its own army and navy. In Africa, the Dutch acquired slaves that could work on the sugar plantations in their South American and Caribbean colonies. The Dutch West India Company owned some 50 ships designated for travel to and from Africa and North America.

PETER STUYVESANT IS BORN

In 1612, Petrus Stuyvesant (his first name would later be Anglicized as "Peter") was born in a region of the Dutch Republic that was almost entirely farmland. He was a peasant, which meant he was a farmer. His mother died when he was 15, and his father, a Calvinist minister of uncommon strictness, remarried. He had one sister, Anna.

Peter, who was stricken with cholera as a boy, eventually left home and lived and studied in the Dutch town of Dokkum, which was a port used by ships owned by the West India Company. He dropped out of college, joined the army, and went to work for the well-known trading company.

NEW NETHERLAND

During the years when Peter Stuyvesant was growing up, West India Company ships began taking settlers interested in making their fortunes in the fur trade to the New World. It took three to four months to cross the Atlantic Ocean, and not long after word of Henry Hudson's death made it to Amsterdam, young couples began making the journey across the Atlantic to settle in the new colony, called New Netherland. In 1623, a ship arrived in the New World carrying some 30 families. Most of them were French-speaking Walloons who were fleeing from religious persecution. Under the rules of the Dutch West India Company, the families had to promise to stay for at least six years. Land was granted based on the size of their family. Another ship, named the *New Netherland,* arrived a year later with 110 people aboard.

Today New York is known for its system of streets and avenues covered in towering skyscrapers, but the geography of New Netherland in those days was quite different. The land was hilly, almost mountainous in some spots, and the coastline was sandy and strewn with oyster shells. A variety of trees covered the terrain, and the dense forests were full of animals like beavers, otters, bears, and deer. The southern tip of the island was a marsh covered in wild reeds. Birds and ducks flew over the heads of the new settlers too. Cows and other animals that could be eaten, however, would have to come by ship from Holland. Documents from the time show that the

The first Dutch settlement on Manhattan Island in 1623 is shown in this illustration. New Netherland was made up of four settlements.

colonists were continuously looking for ways to exploit the land for all its possible economic uses—rivers for boats to sail on, land for farming, and mines rich in minerals.

FOUR YOUNG SETTLEMENTS

New Netherland was made up of four settled areas. Each was near a water source that made traveling, trading with the American Indians, and receiving shipments of supplies much easier. The first settlement was an area at the Delaware River, which the Dutch called the South River. This settlement, which included a tiny settlement called Zwaanendel at the mouth of Delaware Bay, was as far south as New Netherland would ever reach. The second settlement was on an island in the harbor. The Dutch called the island *Noten* Island, or Nut Island, because of the chestnut and walnut trees that grew there. Today it is known as Governor's Island. The third settlement was located to the north around the Connecticut River, which the Dutch named the Fresh River. Finally, there were the settlements that ran up the Hudson River (which the Dutch called the North River). These settlements went as far north as the intersection with the Mohawk River, which has its source at the Great Lakes in the Midwest. Because of the two waterways, it was perfectly located for trading animal furs with the American Indians. This northern settlement included Fort Orange, which today is the state capital city of Albany. All four settlement areas were very small—in the beginning, there were just a few couples sent to each place.

If the voyage over from Amsterdam itself was difficult (many died on board from disease), life in New Netherland was even tougher. There was land to be cleared, homes to be built, and eventually families to be raised. In one such family, a woman named Catalina Trico, married to Joris Rapalje, gave birth to what is thought to be the first person born in New York: Sarah, born in 1626. Millions of descendants of the Rapalje family are living today.

Even more dangerous than the natural elements were the American Indian wars being fought around the settlers. Two tribes near Fort Orange, the Mahican and the Mohawk, despised each other. The

Dutch settlers were drawn into their conflict, and a few of them were killed. The Nut Island settlement saw hard times as well. The director of the colony was suspected of cheating some local American Indians during a trade, and the settlers were fearful the Indians might attack them in response.

After another group of settlers arrived from Amsterdam in 1625, a colony at the southern tip of the island began to develop. This would become the first permanent settlement in Manhattan, called New Amsterdam. Importantly, this group brought 103 head of livestock with them, including sheep, cows, horses, and hogs. The animals were bred so that present and future colonists would have meat to eat. They also brought desperately needed supplies: tools, plows, wagons, weapons, food, seeds, and clothing. One of the men who came over on this trip was an engineer, and soon he laid out a plan of streets and farms for the colony. The farms, called *bouweries,* were large, filled with livestock, and fully functional. They ran lengthwise along both coasts of the island.

PETER MINUIT

What the fledgling settlement of New Netherland needed more than anything else was a leader. For reasons that are not precisely known, the colonists were totally dissatisfied with their first governor, Willem Verhulst. There is historical evidence that he laid down rigid laws and enforced them too strictly. Further, the colonists suspected him of engaging in unfair trades with the American Indians. If the Indians were to ever realize this, the colony could be in danger of attack.

For their new leader, the settlers turned to a man named Peter Minuit (pronounced *min-wee*). Minuit was a Dutchman of French ancestry, and he also spoke German. Back in the Dutch Republic, he was known as a driven and independent businessman. He was anxious to convince the Dutch West India Company to let him sail

Peter Minuit bought the island of Manhattan from a group of local American Indians for tools and supplies valued at sixty guilders.

to the New World. They agreed to let him go, and historians think he may have arrived with the very first settlers. He made trips back and forth and impressed everyone with his energy and ability to lead. By 1626, representatives from the various colonies had formed a council, and they elected Minuit as their leader. He promptly took charge and made an important decision—a decision that resonates to the present day.

Minuit decided that New Netherland, with its four separate settlements, was too spread out. Communication between these groups was difficult, and moreover, it was dangerous. Natives, some of them hostile, were present around all of the settlements, and the threat of attack had become an issue, especially in Fort Orange.

Minuit gathered the settlers together and suggested they all reconvene in one, centrally located place: the island of Manhattan. But he had one issue to resolve before they could make such a big move. He had to buy it.

THE SALE OF MANHATTAN

The story of the American Indians' sale of Manhattan to the Dutch in 1626 for just $24 worth of supplies and tools ranks right up there with other well-known American myths like George Washington chopping down a cherry tree (he probably didn't). In fact, Minuit bought the island of Manhattan from a group of American Indians for supplies and goods worth 60 guilders (the Dutch currency of the time). The $24 figure was determined by a nineteenth-century historian who was researching the sale; $24 is what 60 guilders was worth at the time he was doing his research! So the $24 amount is not only total nonsense, it is historically misleading. Today's historians think that a sale that sounds like the greatest bargain in the history of the world may not have been that different from other American Indian–European land transactions of the day.

Who exactly these American Indians were is not known; many historians think it was probably a group of Lenape. A young Dutchman named Isaack de Rasière, who was serving as the official secretary of the colony, wrote a letter around the time of the sale and referred to a group of *Manhatesen* Indians. In addition to Rasière's letter, historians possess a letter written by a man who worked at the dock in Holland when a ship arrived from New Netherland. In this letter, the dockworker tells his employers of news from the colony: "They have purchased the Island Manhattes from the Indians for 60 guilders . . ." The man's letter is solid proof of both the sale and the cost of Manhattan, though it does not specify which Indians were the sellers.

American Indians did not think land could be "owned" as the Europeans did. Their land was something to barter with, perhaps, but not to sell. Considering this, it is likely that the group of natives that sold Manhattan Island thought they were entering into an agreement with the Dutch along the lines of a treaty or alliance. They were used to doing this with other groups of Indians, in fact. They would align themselves with another group in order to strengthen their numbers in case of hostile attack. Often the sharing of land was part of such alliances. Needless to say, the Dutch (and other European settlers) did not see the deal the same way, and after Minuit's transaction was completed, they felt they owned Manhattan outright. Even after the sale, American Indians continued to live on the island and among the settlers, so ingrained was their idea of sharing the land in the manner of a political alliance.

LIFE IN NEW AMSTERDAM UNDER PETER MINUIT

Peter Minuit and the approximately 200 settlers he governed got to work setting up their life on the southern tip of Manhattan. They named their settlement New Amsterdam, in honor of their home city. Not surprisingly, the colony resembled its namesake: wooden houses, windmills, shops made of yellow bricks, a bakery, a boathouse, and a church.

FORT AMSTERDAM

In addition, a fort was built in the western corner of the colony. Forts were usually built out of logs and were supposed to be a defense against invaders. This fort, named Fort Amsterdam, took 10 years to complete and was finished in 1635. It was not very sturdy: Its four brick walls were reinforced only by dirt on the outside. It constantly needed to be rebuilt. Inside the fort, there was a residence for the governor, living quarters for the officers and soldiers, a small guardhouse, and an office for the colony's secretary. Some historians believe there were residential homes for regular colonists behind the fort's walls as well. Cannons lined the tops of the walls. Also inside was the city's first church, St. Nicholas Church. Built by slaves, it was made of stone. Dutch New Netherlanders were members of the Dutch Reformed Church.

During the early years of New Amsterdam, some of the distinctive features that are associated with New York City began to take shape. For example, a long trail was cleared up the center of the island that would allow the American Indians of the island to travel to the Dutch settlement for trade. Eventually this trail would be enlarged by the Dutch and named the Gentleman's Street; the English would call it Broadway. The city also acquired its first ferry service. In 1638, a ferry began taking residents across the East River between Brooklyn and Pearl Street in Manhattan. Another fascinating thing was happening in those early years—the birth of American multiculturalism. Slowly but surely, ships began to arrive with people who were not only not Dutch, but also not even European. Blacks from Angola, Arabs from North Africa, and Portuguese-speaking Brazilians were arriving, ready to participate in lucrative trades.

As has already been stated, New Netherland was a colony built for doing business and making money. The Dutch tended to mind only their wallets, and so because of this, the colony proved to be rather loose, legally speaking. There were some laws drawn up by Minuit and the government, such as a sundown curfew and restrictions on selling wine, but nothing really stuck, and the colony was largely ungoverned.

FURS AND TIMBER

The colony was, however, doing some rather brisk business, especially in the fur trade. Transactions were done in various currencies: Dutch guilders, wampum (an American Indian currency of polished purple and white beads made from shells), and even in cows that gave milk (which were especially prized). Another industry that grew rapidly in New Netherland was timber. The lands that made up New Netherland, including Manhattan Island, were covered in dense forests of oak and hickory trees. The forests could be cleared and the wood used for building homes, ships, and, eventually, Fort Amsterdam.

Yet the Dutch West India Company was not satisfied. Despite the trade that was occurring, profits were not nearly as high as they

BROADWAY

The first streets of New Amsterdam were created by people walking the same routes to and from their homes and shops every day. Twelve main paths were eventually surveyed, named, and paved with cobblestones. One important street was called *De Heere Straet* ("The Gentleman's Street"), also known as *Heere Wegh* ("Gentleman's Way"), or *Brede Weg* ("Wide Road"). It ran the length of the enclosed city from Fort Amsterdam in the south to the stockade wall in the north. *Heere Wegh* actually followed the path of a Lenape trail named Wickquasgeck Trail that extended up the entire island. Eventually, *Heere Wegh* did too, after a gate was built in the wall. The Dutch widened the street at its southern starting point so that homes could be built along its sides. As it stretched beyond the stockade wall, it became surrounded by farmland. When the English took over New Amsterdam, *Heere Wegh* was renamed "Broadway" and to this very day it runs along the entire length of Manhattan and into the Bronx.

Each of the settlements of New Netherland was located near water and near Native Americans, with whom the colonists could trade. The timber and fur trades were especially lucrative for New Netherland.

would have liked, or even expected. The men running the company quickly realized that if the colony was going to really take off and be a source of serious revenue, it simply needed more settlers living there. They were also losing ground against their competitors. In 1630, New Amsterdam had about 300 residents, mostly Walloons and a small group of slaves. That number improved to 400 by 1638, but as a comparison, the English colony of Boston had 1,000 residents. The Dutch would never catch up: In 1660, near the end of the Dutch rule, the colony would reach 9,000 residents (with 1,500 in New Amsterdam itself), but the English colony in Virginia would hold 25,000, and New England would have 33,000.

A PLAN FOR GROWTH

Like any company, the Dutch West India Company came up with a business plan. Called the Charter of Liberties, the plan allowed wealthy Dutch men (called "patroons," a forerunner of the English word *patron*) to own plantations (called "patroonships") in the New World in exchange for bringing different kinds of workers and craftsmen with them. New Amsterdam desperately needed farmers, bakers, candle makers, wheelwrights, and blacksmiths, and the Dutch West India Company was willing to give land away just to get them there. The deal was that patroons had to transport 50 colonists over a period of 4 years. They were guaranteed enough black slaves so that the settlers would not have to work too hard. It was a tantalizing offer and tough to turn down.

Not everyone associated with the running of the company agreed this was a good idea, and a bitter argument broke out. Peter Minuit was one who thought the idea was terrific; after all, he was head of the colony and wanted to see it develop so that his own influence would grow. Those who opposed the plan were irritated with him and, in 1631, ordered him back to Amsterdam at once. Minuit sailed home and was promptly relieved of his leadership.

4

The English in the New World

At the same time that New Netherland was developing, the English were founding their own colonies in the New World. To the north of the Dutch settlements, two groups of English settlers who were fleeing the religious controversies of their homeland were setting up colonies.

THE PURITANS

The Puritans were a group of Protestants who wanted a complete break from the Catholic Church. Though the Church of England had already severed its ties to Catholicism, it was not enough for the Puritans. They wanted to further "purify" the church. In their spirituality, their lifestyle, and their morals, Puritans were very strict.

Puritans wanted the Catholic hierarchy of popes and bishops to be replaced with a type of church government made up of either church elders or the congregants themselves. Their wariness of authoritarian, Catholic structures bled into their political views. Protestants tended to believe in individual liberties and freedoms. As a philosophical foundation, these beliefs justified their fleeing European monarchies for the New World.

Specifically, the Puritans were under attack in England from supporters of the king, Charles I, who was Protestant but very anti-Puritan. Eventually, in the 1640s, a religious civil war would break out in England, and the Puritans would begin looking to establish a new homeland where they could worship in their own way. They set their sights on North America. In the first five decades of the 1600s, some 60,000 Englishmen moved to the New World.

In the New World, the English had already established a colony in Virginia in 1607. Called Jamestown and led by Captain John Smith, it was the first permanent English settlement in North America. After Jamestown found success with growing and trading tobacco, other English settlements came into being farther north, in an area that Smith named New England.

It is important to note that the Puritans did not establish colonies that allowed the freedom to worship as one chose; one had to be a Puritan. In fact, there were a few New England colonies that were founded by men rejected by the Puritans: Rhode Island, led by Roger Williams, and Pennsylvania, led by William Penn. Williams was ostracized because he was very much in favor of religious freedom as well as the separation between church and state. Penn, on the other hand, was despised because he was a Quaker. Quakerism was an offshoot of Puritanism that was harshly vilified in the Puritan New England colonies.

THE PILGRIMS

One of the most important English colonies in the New World was in Plymouth, Massachusetts. Sailing on the ship *Mayflower* and landing on Plymouth Rock in 1620, the men and women aboard, called Pilgrims, were fleeing religious persecution just like the Puritans. In fact, the difference between the two groups was slight: The Puritans, it is said, were hopeful that the example they set in their New World colony would be emulated back home in England; the Pilgrims were more satisfied starting anew in their own settlement, regardless of what happened in England, and thus are seen as being the more radical of the two.

The Puritans' and Pilgrims' relationships with the Dutch were somewhat complicated. The Pilgrims, before they sailed to North America and landed on Plymouth Rock, actually sought refuge in the Dutch Republic, in the city of Leiden. They were uncomfortable with various aspects of the Dutch way of life and worried that their group would eventually break up if they did not set up their own colony. Once they were in the New World, the Pilgrims and the Puritans had mostly friendly relations with New Netherland; there is evidence that Peter Minuit reached out to the Puritans with an offering of cheese and sugar.

NEW ENGLANDERS IN NEW NETHERLAND

The thriving colonies of New England grew rapidly and by the 1640s held ten times as many people as there were in New Netherland. The New England colonies, which soon included areas of Connecticut, were well organized as well, forming an association called the United Colonies of New England in 1643. The association existed in part to unify the colonies against any future Dutch incursion.

The Pilgrims arrived in Plymouth, Massachusetts, in 1620, after living for a time in the Dutch Republic.

The Puritans, however, were so strict that many New Englanders actually moved south to New Netherland, where citizens could practice whatever religion they wished. The New England refugees were welcomed by the Dutch governor of the time, Willem Kieft, and were even given land on Long Island to settle as long as they swore their loyalty to the Dutch. The English settled cities like Flushing, Southampton, and Jamaica. The cities of Midwout (today, Flatbush), Nieuw Utrecht (New Utrecht), and Breukelen (Brooklyn) were Dutch. Eventually, a treaty was signed in 1650 between the English and Director-General Peter Stuyvesant that divided Long Island into eastern (English) and western (Dutch) halves.

OUTSPOKEN WOMEN

One New Englander who fled England because of her liberal religious views was Lady Deborah Moody. After trying to settle in Massachusetts, Moody, who was already in her fifties, came to New Amsterdam, where Governor Willem Kieft gave her some land in Brooklyn (then spelled Breukelen). She and her friends, who shared her religious views, drew up plans for a community that was the first colony anywhere in the New World established by a woman. Another English woman with unorthodox religious beliefs was Anne Hutchinson, who had been tried and imprisoned in Massachusetts by the Puritans because of her controversial views. She was given an area in what is today the Bronx. It was land populated with hostile American Indians, however, and she and her fellow settlers were attacked and murdered in 1643, not long after they settled there. Today, a river in the Bronx is named for her.

THE ENGLISH AND THE DUTCH IN EUROPE

King Charles I of England also loathed the Dutch. The Dutch Republic was in the middle of a war with Spain and its monarchy. King Charles would ultimately make peace with Spain, much to the annoyance of the Dutch. He hated the Dutch because they were the leaders of the world economy. By the 1630s, the Dutch were first in the trade of spices, sugar, and textiles. Charles wanted England to be first.

Meanwhile, the ship carrying the ousted Peter Minuit was crossing the Atlantic when it ran into a storm and had to land in England. There the ship was held, and the English claimed that they, and not the Dutch, owned the cargo that was aboard. In essence, they were saying that the Dutch had stolen the goods from the English colonies that lay to the north of New Netherland.

Adding to this tension was a violent encounter the Dutch and the English had on the other side of the globe. On an island in the East Indies controlled by the Dutch, some English merchants were killed by Dutchmen in response to a recent English attack. Word of the massacre reached England, and the flames of hatred were fanned between the two countries.

The combination of these events fueled England's dislike for the Dutch as well as its drive to stake a claim in New Netherland. The English were determined to not let the Dutch control North America the way they already controlled the East Indies. The English tried a legal strategy at first. Referring to the landing by the Englishman John Cabot in 1497 on Newfoundland, the English claimed first rights to any settled land in the New World, including New Netherland (never mind the American Indians who were there before either nation). The Dutch, who had of course actually settled the land, refused to recognize England's flimsy argument. The English simply could not back up such a ridiculous claim. New Netherland would remain, for now, Dutch.

Wouter van Twiller succeeded Peter Minuit as director-general of New Netherland. He led the colony for five years, until he was replaced by William Kieft.

After a period with an interim director named Bastiaen Krol, a permanent replacement for Peter Minuit was named: Wouter Van Twiller. History records a mixed picture of Van Twiller. He was known for being corrupt (he claimed for himself a valuable tract of tobacco farmland that belonged to the Dutch West India Company), for drinking too much, and for an incident early in his tenure. Not long after the Dutch fought off England's claim to New Netherland, an English ship sailed into the harbor and indicated that it intended to continue up the Hudson River. The move was in direct defiance of Van Twiller and the Dutch claim on the lands. In an example of his incompetence, Van Twiller let the ship go. It was readily apparent that New Netherland needed someone stronger to replace Peter Minuit.

NEW SWEDEN

Peter Minuit would figure in the story of New Netherland one more time, however. Sweden was watching France, England, Spain and the Dutch Republic wrestle for control of the Atlantic trading routes. Sweden's king, Gustavus Adolphus, had long wanted to compete in the contest for New World trade wealth. He did not live long enough to participate, however, but the Swedish politician who replaced him was friendly with a Dutchman named Samuel Blommaert, who had a position in the Dutch West India Company. Blommaert and his Swedish friend approached Peter Minuit with a bold plan: to set sail for North America and claim some land for Sweden. Minuit knew just where to go: the entrance to the South River (today, the Delaware River), where the Dutch had a fledgling colony.

In March 1638, a tiny fleet of two Swedish ships armed with Swedish and Dutch soldiers sailed into the cape and set up a makeshift colony. It was rough going; by 1640 the colony was barely surviving, and soon the Dutch would move in and swallow it up completely. Nevertheless, a waterfront road in present-day Wilmington, Delaware, is named Swedes' Landing.

PETER STUYVESANT MOVES UP

As they expanded their power in the 1630s, the Dutch sensed that Spain's hold on the Caribbean, and therefore its control of the region's natural resources like salt, sugar, and tobacco, was loosening. They felt that if they could gain control of it, the area could be a key part of the ever-growing Dutch empire. Profitable trade would flow between the Caribbean islands and Manhattan. The West India Company began looking for someone to take charge of their attempt to control the Caribbean Sea.

Not long after he went to work for the West India Company, officials in the company began noticing Peter Stuyvesant's natural leadership abilities. He would make, they thought, an excellent director of the entire Dutch presence in the Caribbean. After officially receiving his position in 1642, the company sent him to various South American and Caribbean locales, including Curaçao, an island off the coast of Venezuela. (To this day, Curaçao remains part of a group of islands owned by the Dutch.) The simple farmer must have been impressed with the South American jungles, climate, food, and native peoples.

Spain was not about to step aside quietly, and there were many fierce battles, including the one in 1644 on the island of St. Martin when Stuyvesant lost his right leg. The war with Spain (and Portugal, which was then under the control of Spain) was unbelievably bloody and violent. It made Stuyvesant tough and somewhat immune to the horrors of war.

5

New Netherland Before Peter Stuyvesant

By the 1640s, the entire island of Manhattan was being settled. While New Amsterdam, with its 80 or 90 little houses and buildings, grew at the very southern tip of the island, other people were setting up large *bouweries* all over the island, including areas that today correspond to Harlem and Central Park. The settlement of Manhattan was not always without conflict, however. A series of violent events dating back to the time of Peter Minuit between the Dutch and the American Indians finally came to a head.

WILLEM KIEFT

Willem Kieft became the new head of New Netherland in 1638, replacing Wouter Van Twiller. Kieft was well connected in Amsterdam, and apparently the West India Company thought him capable enough to lead its New World trade colony. In New Amsterdam, Kieft was a one-man band: Though there was a council of advisors who met to discuss the problems of the colony, the members were close allies of Kieft, and the director had the final word on most decisions. As the settlement was first and foremost a financial investment for the West India Company, keeping the colony thriving economically was the priority. If anything or anyone threatened to disturb the flow of capital, or money, then severe punishments and actions were seen as necessary and defensible. It is interesting to note how different this colony was from the English colonies some 130 years later; the Founding Fathers are remembered as fighting for their independence over issues of democracy and representative government. New Amsterdam at that time was far from a democratic republic. It was more like a monarchy, and Kieft was its king.

CHALLENGES IN THE COLONY

While Willem Kieft succeeded in getting New Amsterdam under control in some ways, such as passing laws about stealing, swearing, arriving to work on time, and selling liquor in stores only, he ran into a number of difficulties almost immediately.

One economic problem Kieft faced right away was the lack of a standard currency. New Netherland did not have a single type of money, and figuring out what goods and services actually cost became very confusing. The problem was even worse once the colony was committed to free trading. Coins from all over the world flooded the shops of New Amsterdam. Interestingly, the currency that had the most usage was American Indian wampum, which consisted of shiny American Indian beads. Willem Kieft tried to make wampum a more standard currency in the settlement to stabilize the local economy.

Meanwhile, the colony's relations with the local American Indians grew worse, and matters were not helped when Kieft, hoping to raise money to support the high cost of running the town, tried to tax them. Local settlers with more knowledge of the Indians than Kieft tried to explain to him that the Indians would never understand, much less agree to, the idea of paying taxes. While the Indians felt that they were part of an alliance with the Dutch, Kieft felt that the Dutch were protecting the natives and that they were owed something for this protection.

KIEFT'S WAR

Kieft apparently was looking for a fight by this point, and he used a small incident involving a stolen pig as an excuse to declare a war on 11 local Lenape groups that included the Tappan, Hackensack, Weckquaesgeek, and the Raritan. It was a horrible and violent war that claimed the lives of 1,600 natives. In 1641, Kieft and his men (whom he had drafted) attacked the Indian men, women, and children in the most gruesome and vicious ways imaginable, including murdering them in their sleep. The settlers of New Amsterdam learned of the massacres and were horrified. The war ended in 1645, and Kieft's popularity in the settlement suffered. An independent council of 12 colonists was formed to advise him, but he usually did whatever he wanted regardless of their recommendations.

Kieft made a key mistake in failing to consider two important characteristics of the Dutch people: They were both tolerant and practical. By this point in their history, the Dutch had experienced many years of religious persecution at the hands of the Spanish and were determined not to act the same way toward others. Further, because New Amsterdam was populated with so many different kinds of people looking to make money in the new trade economy, the Dutch came to tolerate differences in a way that other more

Kieft's popularity suffered when he led a gruesome attack during a war on the 11 local Lenape groups.

homogenous settlements did not. Indeed, many Dutch settlers had taken to learning new skills from the American Indians, for example in farming.

The settlers were furious with Willem Kieft over his treatment of the American Indians. During the war, many colonists had lost their homes, farms, and even members of their family. They blamed Kieft himself—indeed, the war was called "Kieft's War." A new council of advisors was put in place, and they immediately set about challenging Kieft's decisions, including his efforts to raise money for the war by taxing beer. This council was one of the earliest forms of representative government in the New World.

The infuriated colonists began looking for a way to get back at Willem Kieft. There to help them was a young lawyer who would figure prominently in the development of the colony that Peter Stuyvesant was destined to lead. This smart, adventurous Dutchman's name was Adriaen Van der Donck.

ADRIAEN VAN DER DONCK

In 1638, Adriaen Van der Donck began his law studies at an excellent university in the city of Leiden in the Dutch Republic. Leiden was typical of the major Dutch cities of the time—tolerant, multicultural, and teeming with intellectuals and leaders in the fields of art, medicine, chemistry, botany, astronomy, math, and physics. Van der Donck was a fine student and soaked everything up like a sponge. When he finished his degree, it would not have been unexpected for him to practice law or become a judge; after all, he had a law degree from one of the world's finest universities. But Van der Donck listened to his adventurous heart over his intelligent mind and decided to move to New Amsterdam.

RENSSELAERSWYCK

Before he could set sail for the New World, Van der Donck needed a job. Rather than approaching the West India Company, he went to a patroon named Kiliaen van Rensselaer. Van Rensselaer ran a diamond business in Amsterdam and also controlled a 700,000-acre

THE FIRST AMERICANS

When did the word *American* first refer to someone living in the New World? In the 1600s, the word was almost never used to refer to a person, but when it did, it did not mean a European settler. Colonists named themselves based on where they lived: New Netherlanders, New Englanders, or Virginians. Recent study by historians reveals that Adriaen Van der Donck used the term *American* to refer to the American Indians. In addition to the word *American*, the Dutch used *wilden*, which means "natives," and even *naturellen*, which means "people of nature." So when someone says that the American Indians were the first Americans, that's true—literally!

patroonship north of New Amsterdam, near the present-day city of Albany. Though he never saw it himself, Van Rensselaer's colony, named Rensselaerswyck, was large and it surrounded the settlement at Fort Orange, where the fur trade drove the local economy. In fact, the colony was getting so large that it required some kind of governing body to oversee the many farmers, blacksmiths, carpenters, and others whom Van Rensselaer had paid to settle there. Van der Donck's letter inquiring about potential employment was welcome news to Van Rensselaer—the young lawyer was just the kind of man he was looking for. Van der Donck was asked to go to the settlement and work on two problematic issues: negotiating arguments and disputes between the settlers, and pursuing and prosecuting thieves and runaways. He was going to be a *schout*, which is a Dutch word referring to a kind of sheriff. Van der Donck accepted the offer and departed in 1641 on a 10-week journey across the ocean.

PIRACY AND FREE TRADE

Piracy was an issue that every trading company doing overseas business had to deal with. Piracy is the practice of robbing ships of their cargo at sea. It was a difficult practice to police, and no one was immune; Dutch sailors committed their own acts of piracy just as often as they found themselves victims of it. One of the ways the Dutch West India Company combated piracy was by opening up the port of Manhattan in 1640 to trade by other countries. This is called free trade. Suddenly, companies from all over the world could trade with each other, using New Amsterdam as their base. In turn, the West India Company could charge these companies a duty, or tax, to use the port. The men running the Dutch West India Company became extremely rich, and some built fancy homes on Manhattan. Free trade also created a kind of middle class of merchants: people who owned shops like bakeries and taverns, and in turn bought products from other stores. New Amsterdam grew rapidly as a result of free trade—new opportunities for wealth brought new settlers.

Van der Donck, then, arrived at a busy, diverse, and growing New Amsterdam. The nearly 400 settlers were from all over the world and spoke 18 languages. After presenting himself to Willem Kieft, he headed up the Hudson River to Rensselaerswyck, where he would assume his position as leader of the hundred or so colonists living there.

IN LOVE WITH THE NEW WORLD

Van der Donck loved his job. He was totally enamored with the lush new land that he was now in charge of, from its animals and birds to its plants and fruit trees. Yet he knew that New Netherland was sorely in need of laws and policing. As Van der Donck was attempting to create a more civil society, his boss, Van Rensselaer, wanted

This drawing of New Amsterdam was likely made around 1650. In it, one can see one of the two mills that lay outside the walls of Fort Amsterdam. Also visible are the governor's house and St. Nicholas Church, both of which were inside the fort.

him to manage the colony solely as a money-making machine: "It is your duty to seek my advantage and protect me against loss," he commanded Van der Donck in one letter. Trade with non-Dutch colonies was to be restricted, and settlers who were running their own trade deals on the side were to be stopped.

Unfortunately, all the authority that Van Rensselaer vested in Van der Donck went to the young man's head. He soon turned into an arrogant, quick-tempered man and dealt with people harshly and often unfairly. He also defied Van Rensselaer. Their relationship became tense and eventually was almost broken. Van der Donck even tried to set up his own colony, but Van Rensselaer outwitted him—the older man simply bought some of the adjacent land that Van der Donck had his eye on, preventing the young officer from achieving his goal. Eventually, Van Rensselaer died, leaving his colony to his sons. Rensselaerswyck would live on as the state capital city of Albany, and Van der Donck had no choice but to turn his ambitious eye to the south, to New Amsterdam.

PEACE WITH THE INDIANS

Willem Kieft, meanwhile, was being pressured by his employers back in the Dutch Republic to make peace with the Tappan and other local American Indian groups. Kieft agreed to do so. First, he felt, it was necessary to make peace with the Mohawk and the Mahican, who occupied the lands to the north that were under the oversight of Adriaen Van der Donck. Van der Donck knew the ways of these Indians intimately, and Kieft appreciated his presence at the negotiating table. As a reward for his help, Van der Donck was given thousands of acres of land directly north of Manhattan (but still south of Rensselaerswyck), where today the city of Yonkers lies. The peace treaty with the American Indians was successful, but Kieft was still unpopular. He had yet another problem in that the English were moving in on Dutch territory to the north, frightening the colonists who lived up there.

Van der Donck, who by now was offering legal services to the disgruntled colonists, began writing very stern and aggressive letters of complaint to both the West India Company and the States-General in the Dutch capital city of The Hague. In his letters to the government, he demanded more money and support for the colony

as well as recognition of New Netherland as a settlement independent of the West India Company. He also asked for a new director to
replace Willem Kieft.

In response, Van der Donck would be granted only one of his
wishes. The States-General would not allow the colony to be independent, but they would send a new leader. Installing this new leader
would set in motion a series of events ultimately resulting in what
Van der Donck had wanted in the first place: the establishment of
New Netherland as an independent political unit—in essence, the
founding of New York City.

6

Peter Stuyvesant
Takes Charge

Back home in the Dutch Republic, both the merchants
of the West India Company and the politicians in the
States-General were becoming obsessed with the battles
in the Caribbean Sea. The troubles that the colonists
in New Netherland were having with the natives were
minor skirmishes compared to the all-out war in the
Caribbean.

Peter Stuyvesant, ambitious as ever, desperately
wanted to stay near the action, but the condition of his
amputated leg became worse. He decided to go home to
the Dutch Republic to heal. When he arrived, he moved
in with his sister, Anna, who lived near the city of Leiden
with her husband and his sister, Judith. Judith volun-
teered to nurse Stuyvesant's injury, and as it happened,
they fell in love. Judith and Stuyvesant were married,

and his leg eventually healed, though he would walk with a wooden peg leg for the rest of his life.

Stuyvesant was feeling ready to return to the action in the Caribbean. The West India Company, however, had a different plan. Just at the same time that Stuyvesant was asking to be sent back, the letters from Adriaen Van der Donck demanding Willem Kieft's dismissal were arriving. Having proven his courage and loyalty, Peter Stuyvesant was a natural choice for the newest director-general of New Netherland.

ARRIVAL IN NEW AMSTERDAM

When he landed in New Amsterdam on May 11, 1647, Peter Stuyvesant impressed the colonists, many of whom were standing on the shore in anticipation of his arrival. Stuyvesant was "peacock-like, with great state and pomposity," wrote Adriaen Van der Donck. Their new leader wore a metal breastplate and carried a sword. His walk was odd, owing to his wooden peg leg, and his facial expression was serious, like a soldier's. A ceremony was conducted signifying the transfer of leadership from Kieft to Stuyvesant, and then the new director-general and his wife made their way to Fort Amsterdam.

What he found was disgraceful. The fort that he inherited from Kieft was in a state of utter disrepair. Cows were grazing on grass that was growing on the dirt walls, and chickens were scampering about everywhere, even under the cannons. The interior of the fort was also a mess, with soldiers lying about looking dirty, drunk, and hungry.

New Amsterdam itself was not much better. The town's windmills were broken, and one had recently burned down. Vile odors filled the air as outhouses were located right on the streets, which were covered in weeds. The houses were poor looking, not to mention dangerous—most had straw roofs and chimneys made of wood.

Unlike their pious Pilgrim counterparts, the settlers of the New Netherland colony were more interested in making money than in following a moral code. Laws were lax and citizens were loose. Stuyvesant attempted to change the tone of the colony upon his arrival, haranguing those citizens who frequented taverns and avoided church.

Lastly, some 25 percent of the city's buildings were taverns, some-thing the pious, Calvinist Stuyvesant set about changing at once.

His effect on the colony was instantaneous. He immediately set about passing laws and resolutions; among them, a law forbidding the sale of alcohol on Sundays (there had been a rash of drunken fights), and fines for people who fought in the streets or missed attending church. He was equally strict with soldiers, citizens, and employees of the West India Company. Outhouses were moved, buildings were repaired, and farm animals were put in pens. Stuyvesant worked hard each and every day.

THE COLONISTS DEMAND A VOICE

With Kieft's War peacefully ended, the colony began to thrive again. Farms and shops were up and running, and the settlers felt relieved. However, the ill will toward Willem Kieft remained, and it prompted the colonists to ask that their voices be heard in the decision making of the colony. Led by two men named Melyn and Kuyter, the colo-nists demanded some sort of punishment for Kieft, and, in the spirit of Adriaen Van der Donck, they insisted on some representation in their government.

Not only did Stuyvesant flatly refuse both demands, he took Willem Kieft's side in the matter of the former director's treatment of the American Indians that sparked Kieft's War. The colonists were furious. Van der Donck fired off a letter of response to Stuyvesant, demanding again that the colonists be allowed to participate in the running of their own colony. This time, Stuyvesant replied by say-ing that Melyn and Kuyter should be put on trial in Amsterdam. Stuyvesant felt they were being rebellious and treasonous during a time of war (the Dutch were, at that time, still at war with Spain). The two men were ordered to return home, and Kieft, hoping to clear his name with the West India Company, went with them. They would

HARSH PUNISHMENTS

In seventeenth-century New Netherland, punishments were very harsh. Under the strict Calvinist laws that Director-General Peter Stuyvesant laid out, many colonists feared punishment. For example, a colonist caught breaking the law might be tied to a wheelbarrow with chains and forced to do strenuous physical labor for months. Or, one might be given only bread and water to eat. Another form of punishment Stuyvesant favored was tying a person to a cart and then dragging them through the streets of town. "Riding the wooden horse" involved a criminal straddling a wooden sawhorse with heavy weights tied to each leg. In an example of the racism of the time, one punishment was to be forced to work with black slaves for two years. Other offenders were subjected to various forms of torture, such as being tied to a stake, having their heads shaved, having their ears bored, or being flogged. A man convicted of same-sex relations was choked to death in public and his body burned. New Amsterdam also had its own set of public gallows where criminals were hanged to death in front of their fellow colonists.

never make it, however. The ship on which they sailed, the *Princess,* crashed, and Kieft and many others were lost at sea.

STUYVESANT GETS TO WORK

Sure that this was a sign from God that these men deserved the ultimate punishment for their disloyalty to him and the West India Company, Stuyvesant turned his attention to the major issues surrounding New Amsterdam. First were the English settlements to the north. Stuyvesant wanted to make peace with them, not because there was a war raging, but because he sensed that the English were interested in expanding their empire. He and his employers at the West India Company were determined to make New Netherland a permanent Dutch settlement. He began by reaching out to the governor of the Puritan colony of Boston, John Winthrop. Stuyvesant sent a letter to Winthrop, who agreed in a friendly and warm response that the two colonies needed to work out their issues. In 1650, the Treaty of Hartford was signed. It established boundaries between New England and New Netherland.

Next was the issue of Fort Amsterdam. The fort's brick walls were decaying, and the exterior was covered in dirt. Any colonist could have told him that the fort was in a constant state of disrepair. He ordered it completely rebuilt. Further, New Amsterdam was now developed enough where it needed "common buildings," like schools and churches. Then, just as now, building new structures and repairing old ones cost money. In order to raise money from the citizens, Stuyvesant wanted to levy taxes, but the colonists refused. He then tried to tax goods that came in and out of the port, but the lucrative trade to which the colony had become accustomed weakened. Finally, Stuyvesant agreed to the only tax the colonists would accept: a tax on liquor.

THE BOARD OF NINE

Stuyvesant also agreed to the formation of a citizens' council made up of nine colonists who would advise him and make decisions about how their colony should be run. Established in 1652, the council was called the Board of Nine. Adriaen Van der Donck was a founding member and would eventually become its leader. The council did its job well, and Stuyvesant met with members regularly inside Fort Amsterdam.

However, the council soon overstepped its bounds. The membership reiterated the request made many times in the past: that one or two of its members go to The Hague and ask the Dutch government to run New Netherland instead of the West India Company, who employed Stuyvesant. Fearful that such a change would mean he would lose his job, an enraged Stuyvesant tried to ignore the request. But Van der Donck, who was working with the other council members in devising this latest version of his plan, had other ideas.

7

The Fight for New Netherland

The conflict between Peter Stuyvesant and Adriaen Van der Donck would define the early years of Stuyvesant's period in office as director-general of New Netherland. Van der Donck felt he was the voice of the colonists. He hoped to convince the Dutch government to release his beloved colony from the control of Peter Stuyvesant and his employer, the Dutch West India Company. Stuyvesant, on the other hand, was convinced of his own opinion on everything—how to handle the colonists, American Indians, New Englanders, and Van der Donck himself.

VAN DER DONCK'S *REMONSTRANCE OF NEW NETHERLAND*

Adriaen Van der Donck immediately set about to writing a document that thoroughly explained the complaints of the colonists. He would personally deliver it to the government back in the Dutch Republic. It was called the *Remonstrance of New Netherland.* To *remonstrate* means to protest or object to something. It was 84 pages of criticism of the West India Company. For historians, it remains an important primary source from the Dutch colonial era of New York.

THE COLONISTS BUILD THEIR CASE

But first, a remarkable thing happened. Melyn and Kuyter, the two colonists who had been sent back to Amsterdam for demanding representation for the colonists and who had been presumed dead in the

THE NEW NETHERLAND PROJECT

Historians continue to learn new things about New Netherland because of the dedicated work of scholars like Dr. Charles Gehring. Dr. Gehring is the director of the New Netherland Project, created in 1974 and located in the New York State Library in Albany. His project is dedicated to the translation of some 12,000 handwritten documents dating back to colonial Dutch New York. The documents include everything from private journal entries to minutes taken at government meetings. Dr. Gehring can read seventeenth-century Dutch and does all of the translating himself. Of Adriaen Van der Donck's *Description of New Netherland*, Gehring reported, "It has been said that had it not been written in Dutch, it would have gone down as one of the great works of American colonial literature." Gehring is an authority on this period of New York's history and a passionate advocate for crediting the Dutch with the influence they had on America.

crash of the *Princess,* reappeared. Apparently they and a few others had survived the crash and had made their way back to the Dutch Republic, where they reported their experiences in New Amsterdam to the States-General. The government was surprisingly sympathetic and took the side of the colonists and the Board of Nine.

Now armed with written letters of support from the home government, the Board of Nine took another step forward—they went door-to-door in New Amsterdam, asking every single colonist what they thought of Peter Stuyvesant. The council put together a remarkable, detailed document summarizing their neighbors' opinions. In short, the citizens of New Amsterdam were ready to throw out Stuyvesant. Even though Stuyvesant had accomplished much in his short time as director-general, the people were simply tired of not having a strong, permanent voice of their own in the running of the colony. Furthermore, Stuyvesant was a relative newcomer; the weary colonists had been through this before with Willem Kieft.

STUYVESANT FIGHTS BACK

Stuyvesant's reply to the colonists' petition was obstinate and bullying. He searched the home of one of the board members and found a copy of the summary document. Then he ordered Adriaen Van der Donck arrested and put in prison. The other members of the Board of Nine were outraged and demanded that Van der Donck be given a fair trial. Stuyvesant, who had his own loyal committee of advisers, refused. At a town meeting, they went back and forth in dramatic fashion: Melyn attempted to read the letters he had from the Dutch government, but Stuyvesant grabbed them before he could begin, and a fight broke out. Finally, Stuyvesant agreed to release Van der Donck from prison. The director-general had been humiliated. His popularity was extremely low.

VAN DER DONCK IN AMSTERDAM

Free from prison and armed with his *Remonstrance*, Adriaen Van der Donck sailed to Amsterdam in early October 1649. He found a city that was flourishing. The Eighty Years' War between Spain and the Dutch had ended in 1648, with the Dutch winning their independence. Amsterdam, the capital city of the province of Holland, was a booming center of trade, complete with a system of canals that people used to travel within the city itself. Members of its thriving middle class lived in quaint homes with tulip gardens.

The city was also incredibly diverse, both ethnically and culturally. Stepping off the boat that day, Adriaen Van der Donck would have seen Turks arriving with apricots and carpets or Brazilians carrying bricks of sugar, all ready for sale. He would have heard many languages and accents too. And there would have likely been new scientific achievements like eyeglasses and microscopes. It was a golden age of Dutch painting as well; the Dutch master painters Rembrandt and Vermeer were active during this era. Reprints of a painting showing the signing of the recent peace treaty with Spain were flying off the walls of art merchants.

Van der Donck Makes His Case

The people of Amsterdam were still celebrating their independence when Van der Donck arrived, but he was in no mood to have a good time. He moved on to The Hague in the southwest part of the country where the Dutch government, called the States-General, was seated. He presented the legal document that he had written, along with some other supporting evidence. In addition, Van der Donck wanted to make sure that the States-General understood how important it was for the Dutch to hang on to New Netherland, so he had brought as evidence some of the natural resources that were so abundant in the colony. The fruits and grain he displayed were proof of the colony's economic power. Lastly, Van der Donck brought a map and a drawing of New Amsterdam. The drawing was only recently discovered in 1992, and it shows brick and wood houses alongside Fort Amsterdam. The members of the government took their time in considering Van der Donck's case.

Promoting New Netherland

Meanwhile, Van der Donck went looking for more people to come back to New Amsterdam with him. He felt that if he could bring more settlers to the colony, the Dutch government might regard it as a more permanent settlement, agree to take control of it, and push the West India Company out. Van der Donck developed a strategy to stimulate interest in New Amsterdam. Taking advantage of the emerging publishing industry, he found a publisher for his manifesto, the *Remonstrance*. Also published was the map that Van der Donck presented to the Dutch government, and it remains one of the most important historical maps ever created. The citizens of The Hague, Amsterdam, and other Dutch cities were intrigued. In his book, Van der Donck passionately wrote of a heavenly landscape that could be successfully settled and farmed. New Netherland, he wrote, had "very good meadows that could . . . be converted into good tillage [farming] land." He also said the colony's land was "capable of being entirely cultivated by an abundance of people."

People were excited by these descriptions, and many went immediately to the offices of the West India Company to declare themselves ready to make the move at once. The company was surprised by the response, to say the least. As far as it knew, New

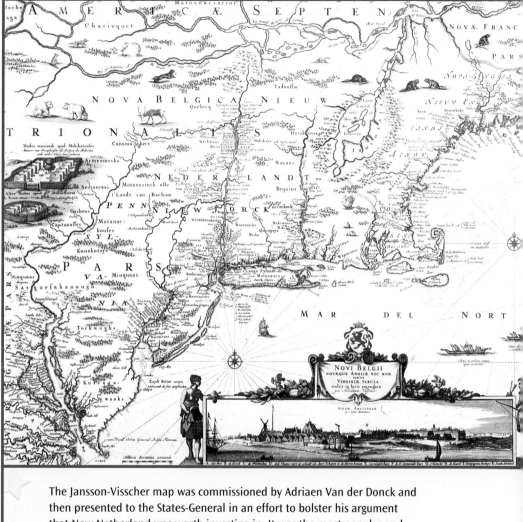

The Jansson-Visscher map was commissioned by Adriaen Van der Donck and then presented to the States-General in an effort to bolster his argument that New Netherland was worth investing in. It was the most popular and important map of the colonial New World for about 100 years.

Netherland was not a place that anyone wanted to go. Soon they had a ship leaving port with 140 settlers on board, all dreaming of owning and farming their own land. Hundreds more would follow shortly thereafter.

THE STATES-GENERAL MAKES A DECISION

Meanwhile, Van der Donck's document was being considered by the States-General. Members were preparing to make a ruling that would have profound effects on the history of New Netherland and, thereby, New York City. It helped Van der Donck's cause immeasurably that suddenly so many people wanted to move there. The States-General sensed that the government could make money in New Netherland just as the West India Company had done.

In April 1650, the government made a ruling in favor of Van der Donck and the Board of Nine. The States-General declared that a municipal government was to be put in place. Van der Donck, feeling confident, pushed further. He asked, in essence, that the West India Company be banned entirely from the colony. The government did not agree to that, but did allow the next boat of settlers to take some guns and ammunition with them so that the colony could defend itself if necessary. It was becoming evident that the States-General was going to take New Netherland seriously. But the government moved slowly, and Van der Donck had to continue to prod them into action over the next few years. In 1652, he made his closing arguments, making the case that the government would be foolish to ignore a place with such great economic potential as New Netherland. He wanted the colony to become an official Dutch possession.

Van der Donck finally got the full-throated victory he wanted: The colony would be totally reorganized under Dutch control. The citizens were guaranteed individual liberties, including freedom of religion. There would also be a "bench of justice," which referred to a court system in which people could be tried under a system of laws. Stuyvesant's personal rule was over. Stuyvesant himself was ordered back to the Dutch Republic to appear before the government's committee. In what must have been an especially delicious victory for Van der Donck, the States-General said that the letter ordering

Stuyvesant to The Hague should be delivered to the director-general by Van der Donck himself. Further, Van der Donck could stay in his role as president of the Board of Nine, and his title was expanded to president of the Commonalty of New Amsterdam. Needless to say, a confrontation between the two men loomed.

Stuyvesant's reactions to the States-General's decisions were typical for him: He angrily threw in prison anyone who disagreed with him; he began spying on members of the Board of Nine; he had people arrested; he seized people's property; and he became generally more strict and stern. Above all else, he felt totally betrayed by Adriaen Van der Donck. He felt especially angry because he was actually doing a lot of good for the colony. For example, he had negotiated boundaries with the English settlers to the north in Connecticut, using both the force of his meager colonial navy and complimentary letters to their leaders to keep the English at bay.

THE FIRST ANGLO-DUTCH WAR

Adriaen Van der Donck was barely getting ready to present Peter Stuyvesant with a letter demanding his removal when, at almost the same moment, war broke out between England and the Dutch Republic. The tensions that had long simmered between the two countries' colonies in the New World were nothing compared with the contempt the two countries held for each other in Europe.

England's new leader, Oliver Cromwell, was fanatically determined that England be the world's most powerful nation. That meant challenging the dominance the Dutch had in world trade—and of course Manhattan was their key port. Cromwell kept his eye on Manhattan and had a great fleet of naval ships built. The conflict got hotter, and the Dutch declared war on England in 1652. Since the reason for going to war was all about who was going to control trade,

The Burning of the Andrew *at the Battle of Scheveningen* (c.1653–4) by
Villem van de Velde the Younger, depicts the final naval battle of the First
Anglo-Dutch War.

it makes sense that the First Anglo-Dutch War was a naval war; it
was fought entirely at sea.

As part of their preparations for war, the Dutch government reconsidered and ultimately reversed all their recent decisions concerning New Netherland. To Adriaen Van der Donck's
supreme irritation, his letter to Stuyvesant was canceled, as was the

decision to bring New Netherland under formal Dutch control. Furthermore, Van der Donck himself was now considered dangerous and suspicious. He was not allowed to return to Manhattan with his family.

VAN DER DONCK'S *A DESCRIPTION OF NEW NETHERLAND*

In the years that followed his unfortunate reversal of fortune, Van der Donck produced a remarkable book called *A Description of New Netherland.* In it he painted a living, breathing picture of the homeland he so desperately missed and loved. In many ways, it is the first great description that historians have of America—its natural beauty is laid bare in loving detail. Furthermore, in his book Van der Donck predicted that Manhattan's population would skyrocket as more and more people from other countries came to settle on its shores. In essence, he unknowingly predicted the massive European immigration to New York of the late 1800s and early 1900s. And, he added, leading the way will be the "compassionate" Dutch people.

Adriaen Van der Donck was finally allowed to leave the Dutch Republic in 1653. As part of the agreement that allowed him to leave, he had to promise to never again hold a political office in New Netherland, nor could he practice law. It was a humbling fall for a man who had come so close to being the leader of New Netherland. That office would remain, for now, in the hands of Peter Stuyvesant.

8

Life in Peter Stuyvesant's New Amsterdam

Peter Stuyvesant, now firmly in charge of New Netherland and its principal city of New Amsterdam, went back to work dealing with the many challenges before him. His position required him to deal with a range of issues, including relations with the local American Indians, complaints from the Dutch colonies beyond New Amsterdam, the encroachment of the New England colonies to the north, and the day-to-day squabbles among residents of New Amsterdam.

THE GROWING CITY

By 1654, New Amsterdam looked a lot like, well, Amsterdam, with cobblestone roads, windmills, schoolhouses, and farms dotting the city landscape. Most citizens lived in townhouses made of brick or stone that had fireplaces and gardens filled with tulips and roses. Wealthier families ate with solid silverware and fine china dishes, paintings hung on the walls, and furniture was made of rare, imported wood. Families of craftsmen lived in simpler wooden homes with living rooms filled with domestic machines that made candles, soap, and butter.

The colony was also seeing a number of significant local improvements, largely thanks to Stuyvesant's firm leadership of the city government that was now in place. For example, to combat the numerous fire hazards in the city, Stuyvesant ordered that straw roofs be made of tile instead, and wooden chimneys be converted to stone or brick. Individual homes were required to have ladders, hooks, and water buckets in case of fire. It was the first example of a fire department.

Around the city, more improvements were noticed. Streets were cleaned and hedges were trimmed. Young children in New Amsterdam went to school at the "Trivial School," which was their elementary school, and a secondary Latin school was also built. There were homes built for orphans and for the poor. The city acquired its first pier in 1648, its first hospital in 1658, and its first post office in 1660. Every Monday there was a big marketplace where townsfolk and overseas visitors could trade homemade goods, crafts, and farm products like cheese, butter, bacon, and turnips. Various sanitary laws were passed as well: Five town garbage dumps were built, and shopkeepers were required to sweep the streets in front of their stores.

For fun, people ice-skated in the winter and raced boats in the summer. Men and women gambled, smoked pipes, and played games such as backgammon and bowling. There were also plenty of rather odd rules that showed Stuyvesant's strict, religious nature. For example, not only was drinking forbidden on Sundays, but so was dancing, going for cart rides, and playing tennis.

Colonists play a game of bowls, an early form of lawn bowling, in seventeenth-century New Netherland. There was time for fun amid the hard work, although Stuyvesant forbade such fun on Sundays.

Just like Amsterdam, a city known for its canals, New Amsterdam had its own canal, which allowed for travel by boat. It was eventually filled in and today is called Broad Street. Men began working as surveyors, planning out the streets and buildings of the city. Stuyvesant oversaw the layout of a simple city grid, and some of the streets were given names. There was no city hall yet—a tavern called *Stadt Huys* ("State House") served as the town meeting place starting in 1642. In fact, taverns were the places where much of the city's action occurred: Government, business, and social meetings took place in these public arenas. (The term *pub*, short for "public house," would be adopted by the English in the 1850s). Because it acted as the city hall, *Stadt Huys* contained a school, courtrooms, and a jail, in addition to the tavern.

LIFE FOR WOMEN

Women in New Amsterdam enjoyed freedoms and privileges that their counterparts in New England did not. Women were allowed to own property, and married women could keep their maiden names. Women had some significant legal rights too. If their husbands were to die, widows in New Amsterdam were allowed to inherit half of the family property and leave the other half to heirs, usually their children. In such cases, daughters could inherit the same as sons. Also unusual for the time was that married women could jointly share some legal rights with their husbands; for example, they were allowed to draw up a will. Wives could even do things such as sue (and be sued), conduct business, and enter into contracts without their husbands being involved at all.

THE PEOPLE AT WORK

The people of New Amsterdam worked extremely hard to keep their little city going. It took every conceivable kind of skilled male worker to make the city function: blacksmiths, locksmiths, carpenters, glassblowers, sailors, sailmakers, tailors, wheelwrights, masons, millers, brewers, soldiers, and farmers. Women ran many of New Amsterdam's shops—the bakeries, trading posts, and even some taverns.

The mills that lay north of New Amsterdam proper were crucially important to life in the city. Built by slaves and run by wind- or waterpower, mills accomplished various tasks. Those that processed grain such as corn, oats, and wheat were called gristmills. Another kind of mill was a sawmill, where logs from the dense Manhattan forests were chopped and cut into planks that could be used to build houses and ships.

New Amsterdam's identity as a major trading port fueled the local economy as well as the kinds of shops and buildings one might see along the streets. The city had a Weighing House where incoming and outgoing cargo was weighed on giant scales offset by huge iron weights. Warehouses were everywhere, filled with foul-smelling animal furs, tobacco leaves, or barrels of ale.

The Dutch kept meticulous records, and a census was first conducted in 1656. A wonderful map exists of New Amsterdam in 1660 that shows every home and building and accounts for every citizen who lived there. It is a fascinating look at where and how the colonial Dutch lived and worked.

NORTH OF NEW AMSTERDAM

Because it was walled in, the city of New Amsterdam became the centerpiece of the entire colony of New Netherland. But directly north of New Amsterdam, behind the fortification wall, lay the rest of Manhattan Island. It was all considered part of New Netherland, and it contained settlers who were more comfortable living in open spaces than in villages or towns. Certain areas were set aside by the Dutch West India Company for official use; a large company farm occupied the west side of the island. It could be very dangerous to live in these sprawling areas on the other side of the wall. An Indian attack could occur at any moment. An early settlement called Haarlem (Harlem today), for example, was overrun by American Indians and had to be rebuilt years later. Other Dutch settlements grew to the east on Long Island as well.

The Dutch settlements farther to the north, such as Fort Orange, lived on. Near Adriaen Van der Donck's old haunting ground of Rensselaerswyck, a booming new town called Beverwyck ("Beaver

Town") grew as a result of the still-thriving fur trade. It was a remarkable place: The local American Indians were welcomed by the residents, and they participated in many of the city's activities. Beverwyck would become Albany, the present-day capital city of New York State.

STUYVESANT'S HOMES

Because he was governor, Peter Stuyvesant had a number of residences. One of his homes was built on land set aside by the West India Company for its director-general on the east side of Manhattan. The governor's estate consisted of about 300 acres that were tended to by 40 black slaves. It was here that Stuyvesant and his wife raised their two sons, Balthazar and Nicholas. Famously, an enormous pear tree that Stuyvesant himself brought back from Amsterdam grew on the lawn in front of the house. The tree stood for some 200 years at the corner of 13th Street and Third Avenue until 1867, when a traffic accident brought it down. It was this home that Stuyvesant retired to after the English took over Manhattan.

His second house, named Whitehall, was made of white stone, and it was located on the very southern tip of the island. Behind it were four beautiful, square-shaped gardens. Stuyvesant paid for the construction of the house himself. The house is long gone, but today, Whitehall Street is named for it. Stuyvesant's brother-in-law lived next door. Finally, there was the governor's house, which was located inside Fort Amsterdam. It was adjacent to the St. Nicholas Church.

A GOVERNMENT IS FORMED

Just because the plan to officially recognize New Amsterdam as independent of the West India Company had fallen through did not mean that its citizens were not going to go ahead with the formation

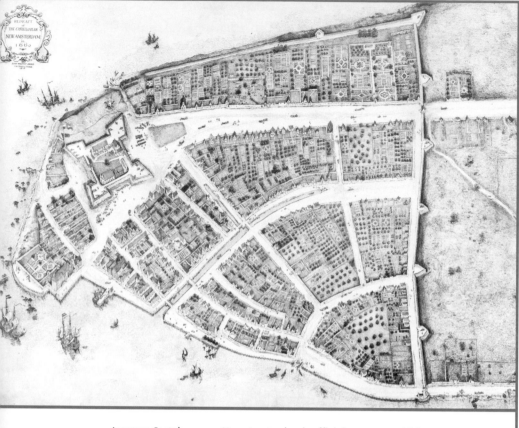

Jacques Cortelyou was New Amsterdam's official surveyor, which meant that he laid out plans for the city and also made maps. His side-view map of New Amsterdam (1660) has given historians a precise idea of how the colony was organized. The four-walled Fort Amsterdam is clearly visible, as is the canal that is today Broad Street. Also prominent is the the street *Heere Wegh*, later renamed Broadway.

of a city government. Indeed, in 1653, a charter was written that formally established New Amsterdam as a city. The municipal government that was set up had one *schout,* or mayor; two *burgomasters* who were in charge of hiring city workers such as fire inspectors and church wardens; and a group of five *schepens,* or magistrates (judges), that served as a kind of city council. Every single one of them was chosen by Peter Stuyvesant. So while some democratic reforms had made their way to the colony, they were only democratic to a point.

One concept that originated in Europe and made its way to Manhattan was the social system of burghers. A burgher was a colonist who could trade his or her (women could be burghers too) goods and participate in the local government. A citizen could become a burgher in one of three ways: by having been born in New Amsterdam, by having lived in New Amsterdam for one year and six weeks, or by paying 20 guilders. Manhattan had two kinds of burghers: those who were very wealthy ("great" burghers) and those who were just plain shopkeepers ("small" burghers). Burghers were shoemakers, carpenters, ministers, military officers, bakers, masons, and chimney sweeps. In this system, when the colony started to thrive because of increased trade, everyone felt the positive effects. And Manhattan was thriving! It was the center of world trade. There were all kinds of new, unfamiliar products, like medicines, writing paper, and citrus fruits, coming in from everywhere. In turn, New Netherland exported furs, beer, grain, and products made from timber. Further enriching Manhattan's diversity, the burgher system attracted even more new settlers looking to get rich from all over the world.

STUYVESANT'S TROUBLES

Stuyvesant's job as leader of New Netherland in the 1650s and 1660s was complicated by the fact that the West India Company wanted to launch naval attacks against England's New World colonies with ships that were docked in Manhattan. This meant, of course, that any retaliation by England would likely involve an invasion of Manhattan. To protect the settlement from possible invasion, the group of magistrates agreed to build a wooden wall across the northern boundary of the city. It was 12 feet high and went from the Hudson

THE OYSTER ISLANDS

When Henry Hudson and his crew sailed into New York Harbor in 1609, one of the many unfamiliar and remarkable natural sights they saw was the local Lenape eating a true native delicacy: oysters. Two tiny islands in the waters surrounding Manhattan were known as Little Oyster Island and Great Oyster Island. Mountainous piles of oyster shells, called "shell middens," covered the shores of Manhattan and the surrounding coastal areas. In fact, the abundance of pearly shells gave *Peral Straet* ("Pearl Street") its name. The two Oyster Islands were littered with oyster beds, and Dutch colonists loved rowing their canoes near them to go "oystering." In the eighteenth century, Little Oyster Island was renamed Ellis Island, known in American history as the place where European immigrants were checked in and examined before going ashore to Manhattan. Great Oyster Island became Liberty Island, home to the Statue of Liberty.

River to the East River. In fact, this is how Wall Street got its name. It began as a wagon road that ran alongside the wall where soldiers stood guard.

Stuyvesant also had to deal with the growing towns on Long Island settled by English colonists who had fled the Puritan New England colonies. These colonists complained to Stuyvesant that thieves and pirates were stealing animals and goods from their property. If they were paying taxes, they argued, they expected to be protected by the city. Predictably, Stuyvesant did not agree with them. Stuyvesant was at odds with the citizens of his colony yet again.

Adriaen Van der Donck, recently returned from the Dutch Republic, was willing to represent the Long Island residents and lodge a formal complaint. Stuyvesant, who blamed Van der Donck for his active role in demanding reforms for the colonists, was not about to permit another uprising, so he denied the request.

STUYVESANT AND NEW SWEDEN

Another issue on Stuyvesant's list was the tiny Swedish colony that lay to the south, along the South (Delaware) River. Still called "New Sweden" and now led by a Swede named Johan Printz, the colony was experiencing tough times. Printz, however, was determined to hang on.

Stuyvesant wanted to get rid of the Swedes once and for all. He dealt with the matter first by ordering the Dutch fort that was there to be repaired, and then for more land to be bought from the local American Indian groups. In this way, Stuyvesant squeezed the Swedish out by controlling all the land around them. Then, fortified with new ships, supplies, and troops from the West India Company, Stuyvesant set out for New Sweden. When he arrived, he confronted the leader of the colony and peacefully won control of the region.

THE DEATH OF ADRIAEN VAN DER DONCK

As Stuyvesant was settling the Swedish matter to the south, he was trampling on someone else's land. The Minqua, the American Indians who lived in the area that was New Sweden, were disturbed by Stuyvesant's presence. They decided to fight back, and they sent word out to groups of natives all over the region. Scores of American Indians from different groups invaded New Amsterdam. They killed a number of citizens and took hostages. The colonists were caught off guard.

The little "war" lasted only a few weeks, but it did claim one key player in the history of New York: Adriaen Van der Donck. Few details of his death are known except that he was likely killed on his farm. Van der Donck left an important legacy: His texts *Remonstrance of New Netherland* and the best-selling *A Description of New Netherland* remain vital documents in the understanding of this period of American history.

9

Different Peoples in New Amsterdam

Despite the leadership that the Dutch demonstrated in areas of individual rights, such as religious freedom and the ability to participate in local government, it would be a mistake to say that New Netherland was a society with liberty and justice for all. Not surprisingly, all of the racial and religious biases of the day lived on in New Netherland. Peter Stuyvesant himself was adamantly opposed to immigration and feared that New Netherland could be become too diverse to rule.

BLACKS

The first 11 slaves of African descent were brought to New Netherland in 1625. At first, slaves were stolen from Spanish and Portuguese trade ships and brought to the island. Eventually the Dutch began enslaving people who lived in their colonies in Brazil and the islands in the Caribbean Sea. Because of this, slaves had names like Anthony Portuguese (the Portuguese were a great trading rival and fought the Dutch for control of Brazil), Van St. Thomas (St. Thomas is a Caribbean island), and Francisco Cartagena (Cartagena is a city in Colombia). After the Dutch lost control of Brazil in 1654, shipments of slaves began to come directly from Africa, and these slaves' names (such as Simon Congo and Gracia D'Angola) reflect their origins as well. Slave trading, in addition to furs and timber, became a major source of income for the Dutch West India Company.

Life for Slaves in New Amsterdam

Private citizens could own slaves in New Amsterdam (by 1664, one out of eight colonists owned at least one slave), but most slaves were owned by the Dutch West India Company, who, somewhat surprisingly, paid them for their hard labor. The company put them to work clearing vast acres of land and building farms, houses, stores, and roads. Not only did slaves build the city wall, but they also cleared the forests and carried the logs that were used to make the structure itself. Without slave labor, New Netherland would have had none of the infrastructure it needed to exist and thrive. In fact, it is not an exaggeration to say that there may never have been a New Netherland for Peter Stuyvesant to govern had it not been for black slaves.

Slaves were active members of New Amsterdam society. They had families, and some black children were educated in schools, sitting right alongside white students. Slaves attended church, too. Baptism in the Dutch Reformed Church became a thorny issue for the colonists. Dutch Reformed ministers were worried that if slaves were baptized, then they might have more cause to claim their

African slaves are auctioned off in New Amsterdam in this engraving.

freedom. As a result, most enslaved blacks and their children were not baptized, and baptism of slaves was outlawed by the church in 1655. During the religious feast of Pinkster (the Dutch Reformed Church's name for Pentecost), blacks both free and enslaved celebrated alongside whites. Slaves were given the day off of work.

Slaves also served as members of the local militia. They played an important role in defending New Netherland from American Indian attacks. Dutch leaders and patroons such as Kiliaen van Rensselaer and Willem Kieft used slaves to ward off American Indian invaders, and Kieft even allowed blacks to settle farms north of New Amsterdam, hoping the farms would act as a natural barrier between the American Indians in the northern part of Manhattan and the city to the south. Called the "Negroes' land," or the "land of the blacks," the farms encompassed more than 130 acres of the island north of New Amsterdam. A list of black landowners of the era has survived, showing the acreage that was granted between 1643 and 1662. These farms were located in what is today Washington Square Park in Greenwich Village. They also became a haven for runaway slaves from New Amsterdam. If a black farmer was found harboring a runaway slave, he was fined.

Half-free Blacks

Eventually there developed a social class of slaves who achieved what was called "half-freedom." Many were granted this status by the Dutch West India Company because, historians surmise, the company did not want to be responsible for the slaves as they aged. Others gained their own half-freedom by petitioning the West India Company, and some tried to achieve it by converting to Christianity, but usually to no avail. By 1650, blacks accounted for somewhere between one-fourth and one-fifth of New Amsterdam's population, and one-third of them were half-free. Though they had a residential home and hospital built for their slaves' use, the company was not charitable toward its former employees: Many half-free slaves were forced to continue to work for the Dutch West India Company even after they were set free, and the company even required half-free blacks to pay a yearly tax consisting of crops that they had raised on their farms.

While the fact that slaves had the possibility of attaining half-freedom was somewhat encouraging, a deep prejudice against blacks persisted in the colony. For example, even if the mother and father in a slave family gained their half-freedom, their children remained enslaved. As the West India Company stated, ". . . children, at present born and yet to be born, shall remain bound and obligated to serve the honorable West India Company as slaves."

In actuality, the West India Company's laws governing New Netherland were not completely clear when it came to slavery; it was not explicitly stated that black people were the only people who could be slaves. Further clouding the picture was that slavery was not recognized by the States-General back in the Dutch Republic. These ambiguities allowed half-free blacks to bring legal complaints regarding their children's status to the city government. Some of these cases went all the way to the States-General in The Hague. In fact, the issue of emancipating the children of half-freed slaves was raised by Adriaen Van der Donck in his *Remonstrance;* however, he had no luck convincing the States-General to change its policy.

Other legal petitions were brought by half-freed slaves regarding pay. Five black men made a case that they should be paid the same as their fellow white workers, who earned eight guilders per month. The company agreed, and the men were paid the money they were owed. As a result of this victory, slaves grew in the esteem of the Dutch officials and were henceforth allowed to petition, or sue. Slaves could also buy themselves or their children out of slavery. Further, there are records of slaves actually being freed by their owners, and even more incredibly, examples of whites going to work for former slaves.

The Economics of Slavery

Peter Stuyvesant, ever the businessman, is on record as having the prejudiced attitudes of the time, saying that slaves should be sold "for the maximum profit of the [West India] Company." Yet he did give official recognition to those who owned property. At one point, the Dutch West India Company encouraged the colonists to train slaves to be skilled workers. The colonists worried that they might lose their jobs to slaves, who were paid less. Stuyvesant, however, said not a chance: "[there are] no able negroes fit to learn a trade."

The slave population of Dutch Manhattan never exceeded 400 (and in fact, some historical sources report a precise figure of 306 blacks brought to New Netherland between 1626 and 1664). There simply wasn't enough of the kind of work that usually ran on slave labor, like cotton plantations or sugar fields, and most tobacco farms lay to the south in the English colony of Virginia.

The real economic benefit of slavery for the Dutch was the money that could be made from the slave trade itself. Many countries that did rely on cotton, sugar, and tobacco had a great need for slaves. Stuyvesant was uniquely qualified to manage these kinds of slave transactions, as one of the lands that needed slaves for its sugar industry was the Caribbean island of Barbados. Stuyvesant had, of course, been director of the Dutch properties in the Caribbean in the years before he came to New Amsterdam, and he retained good relations with many of the merchants there. Slaves were also sold to the English colonies of Maryland and Virginia, the latter being dependent on slave labor for its massive tobacco farms.

THE FIRST AFRICAN AMERICAN

In the years between Henry Hudson's voyages to the New World and the arrival of the first Dutch settlers in 1624, Dutch merchants in the Caribbean were making their own trips to Manhattan Island to trade with the local American Indians. On one such journey, the captain of the ship *Jonge Tobias* left a member of his crew behind, perhaps accidentally, maybe as a result of an argument, or possibly to establish trade with the American Indians. This man was named Jan Rodrigues, and he is generally thought to be the first permanent non–native resident of Manhattan. Rodrigues, who was black, lived on the island and enjoyed successful relations with the American Indians, learning their languages and serving as a translator between the American Indians and the Dutch. He also had a family with a Rockaway woman. Rodrigues was a skilled sailor and owned his own trading post, becoming a successful merchant in his own right.

JEWS

New Netherland was home to a small Jewish population, and it is accurate to say they did not have a champion in Peter Stuyvesant. Despite the reputation for religious tolerance that the Dutch had, Stuyvesant himself was renowned for his loathing of all religions other than Calvinism. He hated Lutherans, Catholics, Quakers, and Jews. As Jai Zion of New York's Lower East Side Jewish Conservancy remarks, think of Peter Stuyvesant not as a "vicious anti-Semite" but as an "equal-opportunity bigot."

A fascinating example of Stuyvesant's intolerance occurred in 1654. A group of 23 Jews living in the Dutch-controlled areas of

Brazil were forced to flee because of the Portuguese Inquisition. In an inquisition, an investigative group is organized to judge whether people are sufficiently religious. In this case, the Portuguese were looking for lapsed Catholics. There were some Brazilian Jews that had converted to Catholicism, but that was not enough for the Inquisition. The lives of these Jews were in danger.

They fled by boat but were captured by Spanish pirates. However, French sailors rescued them and asked them where they were going. "Amsterdam," they replied, but the French took them to *New* Amsterdam. Upon arriving, they kept with Jewish custom and dipped their feet in the waters of the East River.

Stuyvesant was not happy to see them, calling them a "deceitful race." He was afraid that if Jews were let in, then people of all other religions would want to come to Manhattan as well. Never mind that the colony was already populated with people from all over the world; Stuyvesant felt it his duty to keep out those he did not want. He blocked the Jews at every step of the way. For example, the Jews wanted to build a place of worship, and Stuyvesant said no, so they began meeting and worshipping at each other's homes instead. Indeed, the first Jewish synagogue does not appear on a map of Manhattan until 1695, some 30 years after the Dutch relinquished control of the colony to the English.

Asser Levy

There was one man who fought especially hard for Jewish rights in Manhattan. His name was Asser Levy. He was a butcher, and in one of his early fights with Stuyvesant, he asked to be allowed to prepare kosher meat, in keeping with the Jewish religion. Stuyvesant refused and defended himself by saying (ironically) that Levy should be a butcher for everyone, not just for Jews. Of course Stuyvesant was ignoring those Jews who could only eat kosher meat.

In this lithograph, Peter Stuyvesant chastises Willem Wickendam for preaching a Baptist sermon. Stuyvesant was intolerant of views that differed from his own.

Levy also fought Stuyvesant on matters of Jewish citizenship in the city. The director-general did not want Jews to carry any of the responsibilities of the rest of the citizenry for fear they would eventually want full civil rights. After the defense wall was built along the northern border of the city, every citizen had to take turns patrolling during the night. During guard duty, one carried a long wooden rattle that could be shaken if there were danger—an Indian invasion, for example. Then everyone would be awakened by the noise and defend the city. Many citizens did not like doing guard duty, and Levy offered to take their shifts. By doing so, Levy felt he had done a duty that entitled him to be a citizen. Levy took his case all the way to the States-General in the Dutch Republic and won his case. Jews were allowed to perform guard duty and were eventually allowed to be burghers like everyone else.

QUAKERS AND LUTHERANS

Stuyvesant was determined to keep New Amsterdam purely Calvinist. As with the Jews, he issued orders blocking Lutherans from worshipping for fear that their inclusion might encourage other religions to take hold in the colony. He even threw some Lutherans in jail for worshipping in defiance of his order.

He also opposed the Quakers. Quakerism was another offshoot of Puritanism, and Quakers worshipped in such a passionate way that they sometimes trembled, or "quaked," as they prayed and celebrated their faith. Rejected by the Puritans in New England, they had come south to the Long Island town of Vlissingen because of New Netherland's reputation for religious tolerance. They were in for a surprise. Peter Stuyvesant felt they were likely to make trouble in his colony and oversaw the torture and persecution of Quakers personally. He also told the citizens of Vlissingen not to support what he saw as a crazy, fanatical group. The Quakers filed a formal complaint, citing the Dutch Republic's constitutional belief in religious tolerance. Their protest, called the Flushing Remonstrance, was met with stern opposition from Stuyvesant. He arrested people and threw them in prison. But the deed was done; the Flushing Remonstrance is remembered as an important moment in the development of religious freedom in the United States.

10

England and New York

By the late 1650s, the Dutch West India Company was losing faith in Peter Stuyvesant. They were upset that he had such poor relations with the New Netherland colonies outside New Amsterdam. The city was in good shape, but the outlying areas were not. Their citizens, who it must be remembered were mostly English refugees, wanted to go back to New England, despite the strict religious practices that had caused them to flee.

TWO COMPETING PLANS

The First Anglo-Dutch War ended in 1654 when the Dutch made peace with Oliver Cromwell, the English leader. After the death of Cromwell in 1658, a king, Charles II, was once again in charge of England. During this period, two Englishmen important to the future of New Netherland emerged: George Downing and John Winthrop.

George Downing was a grouchy, aggressive man who was serving as England's representative in the Dutch Republic. John Winthrop shared his name with his father, the governor of the Puritan colony of Boston. John Winthrop the Younger, as he was called, was governor of Connecticut. Winthrop went to see Charles II to secure a formal charter for his colony. A charter is an official document that defines the boundaries and rights of a colony or city. Winthrop kept his ambitions quiet, but soon it became known that he wanted all the land south of Massachusetts to Virginia, and as far west as the Pacific Ocean. This included, of course, all of the land occupied by New Netherland. The king granted his wish, and as a result, a major political conflict was created: The governor of an English colony now had formal claim (at least from *his* country) to New Netherland. Complicating this was the fact that Peter Stuyvesant and John Winthrop were friends. Winthrop had to handle this aspect of his ambitions delicately. As he considered this, he and his Connecticut colony started moving in on New Netherland from the north.

At the same time, George Downing was urging King Charles II to wake up and smell the coffee, literally: The Dutch had become wildly rich by controlling the Caribbean trade of coffee as well as other goods. Downing wanted part—or all—of that industry. He knew that not only was Manhattan prized as a trade port, but the Hudson River, running along the island's west side, also served as a northerly and westerly route to the rest of North America. If what the English had seen so far of the New World was any indication of what else might lie on the continent, then, they surmised, there had to be astonishing riches to be made by controlling as much North American land as possible. Controlling New Netherland meant controlling the Hudson River.

By tempting him with the image of a land of plenty, Downing convinced the king's brother, James Stuart, who was in charge of the navy, to support an invasion of New Netherland. Downing also came up with his own plan for English possession of the entire Atlantic Coast—a plan that challenged the Connecticut charter of John Winthrop. In March 1664, King Charles II went with Downing's plan and formally gave the lands from the present-day states of Maine to Delaware as a gift to his brother James Stuart, the duke of York. An invasion of New Netherland was ordered.

THE ENGLISH INVADE

Richard Nicolls, an English sailor, led a fleet of four ships armed with 450 soldiers to New England. Nicolls first told a crestfallen John Winthrop that his plan for an expansion of Connecticut was being dropped. He then prepared to move southward to New Netherland. George Downing was in contact with the States-General in the Dutch Republic and told them that, yes, the English were sending a fleet of ships across the Atlantic, but, no, the Dutch had nothing to fear. At peace with England since the end of the First Anglo-Dutch War, the Dutch politicians in Amsterdam did not suspect that the invasion was a hostile act.

Peter Stuyvesant, however, had been given a warning by an English friend and ordered New Amsterdam to prepare for an invasion. At the moment of invasion, Stuyvesant was upriver dealing with a situation involving the Mohawk. He raced home and found his citizens frightened and confused.

It was August 26, 1664, and Nicolls, standing on a ship docked in the harbor, first sent a letter to Stuyvesant on shore demanding he turn over Manhattan to England. Receiving no answer, John Winthrop and a few other men rowed a boat ashore, and a meeting was

Colonists plead with Stuyvesant not to open fire on the British who have arrived in warships waiting in the harbor to claim the territory for England. The colonists had had enough of their leader and they did not want to go to war with England.

arranged at a nearby tavern. There they handed Stuyvesant another letter from Nicolls describing an extremely generous offer.

At some later point, officials in the New Amsterdam government asked to read the offer, but Stuyvesant just tore up the paper and vowed to fight to the end. With that, the colonists had had enough. They were fed up with Stuyvesant and his bullying. His autocratic ways, always in the name of following orders from the West India Company, had finally worn out their welcome. He was committing

them to a war that they did not want to fight—and one that was to
be fought in the name of loyalty to a company that they loathed and
resented. The answer was no; they were not going to go to war with
England. It soon emerged that everyone was against him, including
his own 17-year-old son. Ninety-three of the most prominent members of New Amsterdam society signed a petition demanding Stuyvesant accept the generous English terms of surrender. Very reluctantly,
he did. The day had finally arrived when the control of these colonists'
lives would transfer to another world power: the English. Named for
the duke of York, the king's brother, New York was born.

THE ARTICLES OF CAPITULATION

The story does not end there, however. The Dutch colonists did not
disappear just because the English were in charge; in fact they were
allowed to continue living just as they had before. Further, Peter
Stuyvesant did not leave, either. Richard Nicolls, the leader of the
English invasion, succeeded Stuyvesant as director-general. An official transfer of power from Stuyvesant to Nicolls took place on Sep-
tember 6, 1664, at Stuyvesant's farmhouse north of the walled city.
In the document, known as the Articles of Capitulation, some spe-
cific freedoms for the Dutch citizenry were guaranteed, including
"liberty of their Consciences." It is a vague term, but it is assumed
that it included the freedoms the colonists were accustomed to, such
as freedom of religion and the right to be represented in the local
government. Interestingly, there is evidence that it was Stuyvesant who directed the English to include such language. While it
is remarkable that the English agreed to the document, it is truly
astonishing that the strict, dictatorial Peter Stuyvesant would have
insisted that such language be included. Perhaps 17 years at the
helm of a diverse colony had taught him that citizens of a colony

would eventually demand their individual rights. Why not secure them from the beginning?

Today, history appreciates the Articles of Capitulation as part of the legacy of the Dutch colonial period; freedom of religion is guaranteed in the U.S. Constitution. Unfortunately, the freedoms that Stuyvesant sought for his people did not extend to slaves. As part of the articles, Stuyvesant and Nicolls agreed that slavery would continue in Manhattan under British rule.

PETER STUYVESANT GOES HOME

Peter Stuyvesant was ordered to return to Amsterdam to stand trial. The States-General were thinking about punishing him for surrendering to the English. In the end, he was spared any punishment and allowed, at his own request, to return to his farm in newly named New York. Considering that it was a place that he hardly got any joy from, it is notable that Stuyvesant wanted to spend his remaining days there. In his final years, he seemed to actually acquire some affection from his fellow Manhattanites; when they saw him on the street, they called him "the General." Stuyvesant lived his remaining years on his *bouwerie* with his wife, sons, and slaves, and was in his early sixties when he died in 1672.

PETER STUYVESANT'S LEGACY

For many years, Peter Stuyvesant was remembered by history as a kind of cartoon character—a crotchety old man with a wooden leg. More recent scholarship, however, has revealed a man not without considerable faults, but whose strong, determined leadership brought many changes that the citizens of New Amsterdam came to appreciate, such as making New Amsterdam a cleaner, safer place to live. Yet

A statue of Stuyvesant is located in the yard of St. Mark's in the Bowery Church in Manhattan. The church stands on the site of the chapel on Stuyvesant's farm. He and many of his descendants are buried on the site.

despite his successes, his autocratic ways, his unyielding allegiance to his employer, and his acts of virulent racism and religious intolerance have not allowed his reputation to improve very much over time.

Today, a number of places are named for him in New York. A statue of him stands in Stuyvesant Square, and there is a primarily African-American neighborhood in Brooklyn called Bedford-Stuyvesant. Stuyvesant Town is the name of a group of private, luxury apartment buildings not far from where he lived on his *bou-werie,* and Stuyvesant High School is a very prestigious math, science, and technology public high school across from the site of the former World Trade Center in Lower Manhattan.

FURTHER CONFLICTS

The transfer of New Netherland to the English did not put an end to the tensions between England and the Dutch. In fact, it inflamed them. A Second Anglo-Dutch War broke out as a result of the takeover—a war in which, interestingly enough, the Dutch were the victors. Somewhat strangely, in the treaty ending the war, the Dutch did not ask for New York back.

But that was still not the end of things. A Third Anglo-Dutch War occurred just five years later, and this time, the Dutch sailed their fleet right into New York Harbor and claimed Manhattan for themselves once again. Yet 15 months later, the Dutch gave it all back to England as part of a lasting, final peace treaty between the two nations. Trade with the Dutch continued unabated, and the English finally controlled a city that was the incorporation of two great trading empires.

THE DUTCH LEGACY

Though they only controlled the area around Manhattan and the Hudson River for about 40 years, the Dutch made a considerable impact on both New York and America. Most importantly, Dutch attitudes (though not Peter Stuyvesant's attitude) toward religious freedom were a foundation that the Founding Fathers stood on when crafting the U.S. Bill of Rights. Further, when the New York City charter was established in 1668, it included those rights that the Dutch had insisted upon in the Articles of Capitulation. Another important

A TASTY HERITAGE

Three very American foods actually have their origins in Dutch cuisine. Coleslaw began in New Amsterdam when cooks cut up cabbage and mixed it with vinegar or melted butter. The word *cookie* is based on the Dutch word *koeckjes*, which means "little cakes." The cookie itself was not Dutch—English biscuits are the forerunners of cookies—but the word is Dutch. Finally, the waffles that Americans enjoy for breakfast have their origin in Holland. The Pilgrims likely brought them over with them after living in Leiden.

characteristic of New Amsterdam was its cultural pluralism. From its earliest days, New Amsterdam was a multicultural melting pot of different peoples. The cultural and ethnic diversity that New York is famous for was present from its beginnings. Yet another legacy of the Dutch colonial era was its emphasis on trade and commerce. Today, New York is the world's financial capital. It had its start as the main trade hub of the Dutch West India Company.

NEW YORK TODAY

In terms of physical evidence, there is little that remains of the Dutch colonial period in New York. If you travel to Pearl Street in Lower Manhattan, a few bricks from the old *Stadt Huys* tavern and city hall can be seen through a small window in the street. Also, the haphazard way the streets of Lower Manhattan are laid out is a remnant of New Amsterdam. And of course, some of the street names in Manhattan, such as Whitehall Street, Pearl Street, and the Bowery, have their origins in the Dutch language.

While this story has been mostly about Peter Stuyvesant, many historians are reexamining the contribution of his great rival, Adriaen Van der Donck. After all, Van der Donck's vision of Manhattan as a multinational, religiously diverse community has endured. As author Russell Shorto has put it, "What matters about the Dutch colony is that it set Manhattan on a course as a place of openness and free trade." It is a place that millions of people live in, visit, and enjoy today.

Chronology

1609	Henry Hudson sails the *Half Moon* into New York Harbor.
1612	Peter Stuyvesant born in the Netherlands.
1623	First permanent colonists sail to New Netherland.
1625	First black slaves arrive in New Amsterdam.

TIMELINE

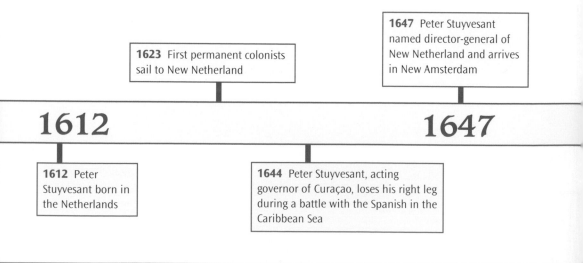

1623 First permanent colonists sail to New Netherland

1647 Peter Stuyvesant named director-general of New Netherland and arrives in New Amsterdam

1612

1647

1612 Peter Stuyvesant born in the Netherlands

1644 Peter Stuyvesant, acting governor of Curaçao, loses his right leg during a battle with the Spanish in the Caribbean Sea

1626	Peter Minuit purchases the island of Manhattan from a group of Native Americans.
1635	Fort Amsterdam completed.
1641–45	Kieft's War.
1644	Peter Stuyvesant, acting governor of Curaçao, loses his right leg during a battle with the Spanish in the Caribbean Sea.
1647	Peter Stuyvesant named director-general of New Netherland and arrives in New Amsterdam.
1648	The Dutch win independence from Spain.
1649	Adriaen Van der Donck asks the States-General in the Netherlands for reforms in New Amsterdam.

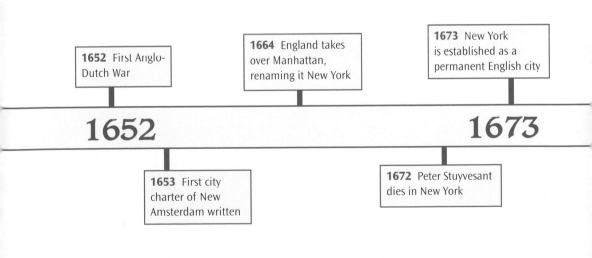

1652 First Anglo-Dutch War

1664 England takes over Manhattan, renaming it New York

1673 New York is established as a permanent English city

1652

1673

1653 First city charter of New Amsterdam written

1672 Peter Stuyvesant dies in New York

1652	First Anglo-Dutch War.
1653	First city charter of New Amsterdam written.
1664	England takes over Manhattan, renaming it New York.
1672	Peter Stuyvesant dies in New York.
1673	The Dutch retake New York as part of Third Anglo-Dutch War; 15 months later, a peace treaty is signed between England and the Dutch; New York is established as a permanent English city.

Bibliography

Amsterdam/New Amsterdam: The Worlds of Henry Hudson. Exhibition curated by Dr. Sarah M. Henry. New York: Museum of the City of New York, 2009.

Berlin, Ira, and Leslie M. Harris, eds. *Slavery in New York.* New York: The New Press, 2005.

Burns, Ric. *New York: A Documentary Film.* Episode 1, "The Country and the City: 1609–1825," 1999.

Burns, Ric, and James Sanders, with Lisa Ades. *New York: An Illustrated History.* New York; Alfred A. Knopf, 1999.

Burrows, Edwin G., and Mike Wallace. *Gotham.* New York: Oxford University Press, 1999.

City-Data.com. "New York – Religions." Available online. URL: http://www.city-data.com/states/New-York-Religions.html (accessed June 2, 2009).

Cohen, Paul E., and Robert T. Augustyn. *Manhattan in Maps, 1527–1995.* New York: Rizzoli, 1997.

Davis, Lavinia R. *Island City.* Garden City, New York: Doubleday & Company, 1961.

Deák, Gloria. *Picturing New York.* New York: Columbia University Press, 2000.

Dictionary.com, s.v. "charter," http://dictionary.reference.com/browse/charter (accessed May 1, 2009).

Encyclopaedia Britannica Online, s.v. "Anglo-Dutch Wars," http://search.eb.com/eb/article-9007585 (accessed May 1, 2009).

_____, s.v. "Cabot, John," http://search.eb.com/eb/article-9018457 (accessed May 1, 2009).

_____, s.v. "Calvin, John," http://search.eb.com/eb/article-9106115 (accessed May 1, 2009).

_____, s.v. "Calvinism," http://search.eb.com/eb/article-9106116 (accessed May 1, 2009).

_____, s.v. "Columbus, Christopher," http://search.eb.com/eb/article-9109621 (accessed May 1, 2009).

_____, s.v. "Delaware," http://search.eb.com/eb/article-9085966 (accessed May 1, 2009).

_____, s.v. "Dutch East India Company," http://search.eb.com/eb/article-9031608 (accessed May 1, 2009).

_____, s.v. "Dutch Republic," http://search.eb.com/eb/article-9031616 (accessed May 1, 2009).

_____, s.v. "Dutch West India Company," http://search.eb.com/eb/article-9031618 (accessed May 1, 2009).

_____, s.v. "Eighty Years' War," http://search.eb.com/eb/article-9032141 (accessed May 1, 2009).

_____, s.v. "Flemings and Walloons," http://search.eb.com/eb/article-9034547 (accessed May 1, 2009).

_____, s.v. "Holland," http://search.eb.com/eb/article-9040788 (accessed May 1, 2009).

_____, s.v. "Hutchinson, Anne," http://search.eb.com/eb/article-9041641 (accessed May 1, 2009).

_____, s.v. "ice age," http://search.eb.com/eb/article-9041958 (accessed May 1, 2009).

_____, s.v. "Jamestown Colony," http://search.eb.com/eb/article-9043322 (accessed May 1, 2009).

_____, s.v. "Lewes," http://search.eb.com/eb/article-9048010 (accessed May 1, 2009).

_____, s.v. "Long Island," http://search.eb.com/eb/article-9048857 (accessed May 1, 2009).

_____, s.v. "Luther, Martin," http://search.eb.com/eb/article-9108504 (accessed May 1, 2009).

_____, s.v. "Massachusetts," http://search.eb.com/eb/article-9111239 (accessed May 1, 2009).

_____, s.v. "Minuit, Peter," http://search.eb.com/eb/article-9052900 (accessed May 1, 2009).

————, s.v. "Muscovy Company," http://search.eb.com/eb/article-90 54408 (accessed May 1, 2009).

————, s.v. "New England," http://search.eb.com/eb/article-9055457 (accessed May 1, 2009).

————, s.v. "New York: History: Colonial Period," http://search. eb.com/eb/article-78270 (accessed May 1, 2009).

————, s.v. "Northwest Passage," http://search.eb.com/eb/article-90 56285 (accessed May 1, 2009).

————, s.v. "Pilgrim Fathers," http://search.eb.com/eb/article-90 60020 (accessed May 1, 2009).

————, s.v. "Polo, Marco," http://search.eb.com/eb/article-9060660 (accessed May 1, 2009).

————, s.v. "Puritanism," http://search.eb.com/eb/article-9061955 (accessed May 1, 2009).

————, s.v. "Quaker," http://search.eb.com/eb/article-9062149 (accessed May 1, 2009).

————, s.v. "Smith, John," http://search.eb.com/eb/article-9068287 (accessed May 1, 2009).

————, s.v. "Stuyvesant, Peter," http://search.eb.com/eb/article-90 70067 (accessed May 1, 2009).

————, s.v. "tobacco," http://search.eb.com/eb/article-9111043 (accessed May 1, 2009).

————, s.v. "Verrazzano, Giovanni da," http://search.eb.com/eb/ article-9075141 (accessed May 1, 2009).

————, s.v. "waffle," http://search.eb.com/eb/article-9075836 (accessed May 1, 2009).

————, s.v. "Wallonia," http://search.eb.com/eb/article-9002838 (accessed May 1, 2009).

————, s.v. "wampum," http://search.eb.com/eb/article-9076035 (accessed May 1, 2009).

————, s.v. "Winthrop, John," http://search.eb.com/eb/article-90 77241 (accessed May 1, 2009).

Garraty, John A., and Peter Gay, eds. *The Columbia History of the World.* New York: Harper & Row, 1972.

Gotham Center for New York History. Available online. URL: http://www.gothamcenter.org/ (accessed June 2, 2009).

Harris, Leslie M. *In the Shadow of Slavery.* Chicago: The University of Chicago Press, 2003.

The History Enthusiast. "Did Washington Chop Down that Cherry Tree?" Available online. URL: http://historyenthusiast.blogspot. com/2006/07/did-washington-chop-down-that-cherry.html (accessed May 1, 2009).

Hodges, Graham Russell. *Root & Branch.* Chapel Hill: The University of North Carolina Press, 1999.

Homberger, Eric. *The Historical Atlas of New York City.* Rev. ed. New York: Henry Holt and Company, 2005.

Hühner, Cyrus Adler L. "Asser Levy (Asser Levy van Swellem)." www. jewishencyclopedia.com Available online. URL: http://www. jewishencyclopedia.com/view.jsp?artid=310&letter=L (accessed June 2, 2009).

Kaufman, Terry. "Waffles - Contemporary Food with Thousands of Years of History." Available online. URL: http://ezinearticles. com/?Waffles—-Contemporary-Food-with-Thousands-of-Years-of-History&id=967437 (accessed online June 2, 2009).

Kenney, Alice P. *Stubborn for Liberty.* Syracuse, N.Y.: Syracuse University Press, 1975.

Kessler, Henry H., and Eugene Rachlis. *Peter Stuyvesant and His New York.* New York: Random House, 1959.

Klein, Milton M., ed. *The Empire State.* Ithaca, N.Y.: Cornell University Press, 2001.

Knopf Guides. *New York.* 3rd ed. New York: Alfred A. Knopf, 1996.

Kurlansky, Mark. *The Big Oyster.* New York: Random House, 2006.

Lobel, Arnold. *On the Day Peter Stuyvesant Sailed into Town.* New York: Harper & Row, 1971.

Logan, Samuel T., Jr. "The Pilgrims and Puritans: Total Reformation for the Glory of God." www.puritansermons.com Available online. URL: http://www.puritansermons.com/banner/logan1.htm (accessed June 2, 2009).

MAAP: Mapping the African American Past. Available online. URL: http://www.maap.columbia.edu/ (accessed June 2, 2009).

Meinig, D.W. *The Shaping of America.* New Haven, Conn.: Yale University Press, 1986.

New Netherland Project. Available online. URL: http://www.nnp.org/ (accessed June 2, 2009).

New York State Archives. Available online. URL: http://www.archives. nysed.gov (accessed June 2, 2009).

The New York Times. *The New York Times Guide to Essential Knowledge.* 2nd ed. New York: St. Martin's Press, 2007.

The New York Times. "Untimely End of the Stuyvesant Pear Tree." February 27, 1867. Available online. URL: http://query.nytimes. com/mem/archive-free/pdf?_r=1&res=9E00E5D9133AEF34BC 4F51DFB466838C679FDE (accessed June 2, 2009).

The Papers of George Washington. "Frequently Asked Questions." Available online. URL: http://gwpapers.virginia.edu/project/faq/ index.html (accessed May 1, 2009).

Quackenbush, Robert. *Old Silver Leg Takes Over!* Englewood Cliffs, N.J.: Prentice-Hall, 1986.

Shorto, Russell. *The Island at the Center of the World.* New York: Vintage Books, 2004.

Spier, Peter. *The Legend of New Amsterdam.* Garden City, N.Y.: Doubleday & Company, 1979.

Stuyvesant High School. Available online. URL: http://stuy.edu (accessed June 2, 2009).

Stuyvesant Town. Available online. URL: http://www.stuytown. com/#/home (accessed June 2, 2009).

Taylor, Alan. *American Colonies.* New York: Penguin Books, 2001.

Taylor, Dale. *The Writer's Guide to Everyday Life in Colonial America.* Cincinnati: Writer's Digest Books, 1997.

Trager, James. *The New York Chronology.* New York: HarperCollins Publishers, 2003.

Tunis, Edwin. *Colonial Living.* Cleveland: The World Publishing Company, 1957.

U.S. Census Bureau. "State & County QuickFacts: New York (City), New York." Available online. URL: http://quickfacts.census.gov/ qfd/states/36/3651000.html (accessed June 2, 2009).

Van der Zee, Henri, and Barbara. *A Sweet and Alien Land.* New York: The Viking Press, 1978.

Widdemer, Mabel Cleland. *Peter Stuyvesant: Boy with Wooden Shoes.* Indianapolis, Ind.: The Bobbs-Merrill Company, 1950.

Zion, Jai. Remarks given on walking tour of the Financial District of New York City, May 17, 2009. Jewish Tours of New York in Lower East Side, sponsored by the Lower Eastside Jewish Conservancy.

Further Resources

BOOKS

Berlin, Ira, and Leslie M. Harris, eds. *Slavery in New York*. New York: The New Press, 2005.

Burns, Ric, and James Sanders, with Lisa Ades. *New York: An Illustrated History*. New York; Alfred A. Knopf, 1999.

Burrows, Edwin G., and Mike Wallace. *Gotham*. New York: Oxford University Press, 1999.

Deák, Gloria. *Picturing New York*. New York: Columbia University Press, 2000.

Harris, Leslie M. *In the Shadow of Slavery*. Chicago: The University of Chicago Press, 2003.

Hodges, Graham Russell. *Root & Branch*. Chapel Hill.: The University of North Carolina Press, 1999.

Homberger, Eric. *The Historical Atlas of New York City*. Rev. ed. New York: Henry Holt and Company, 2005.

Kenney, Alice P. *Stubborn for Liberty*. Syracuse, N.Y.: Syracuse University Press, 1975.

Kessler, Henry H., and Eugene Rachlis. *Peter Stuyvesant and His New York*. New York: Random House, 1959.

Klein, Milton M., ed. *The Empire State*. Ithaca, N.Y.: Cornell University Press, 2001.

Rink, Oliver A. *Holland on the Hudson*. Ithaca, N.Y.: Cornell University Press, 1986.

Shorto, Russell. *The Island at the Center of the World*. New York: Vintage Books, 2004.

Taylor, Alan. *American Colonies*. New York: Penguin Books, 2001.

Van der Zee, Henri, and Barbara. *A Sweet and Alien Land.* New York: The Viking Press, 1978.

FILM

Dutch New York. A production of Thirteen in association with WNET.org. Produced by James Nicoloro. 2009.

WEB SITES

Gotham Center for New York History
  http://www.gothamcenter.org/

MAAP: Mapping the African American Past
  http://www.maap.columbia.edu/

New Netherland Museum
  http://www.newnetherland.org/

New Netherland Project
  http://www.nnp.org/

Picture Credits

76: Redraft of The Castello
Plan, New Amsterdam in
1660, 1916, Adams, John
Wolcott (1874–1925)/
Collection of the New-York
Historical Society, USA/
The Bridgeman Art Library
International

83: Dutch auction of African
slaves in New Amsterdam
(later New York City) 1643
(engraving), American
School, (17th century)/
Private Collection / Peter

Newark American Pictures/
The Bridgeman Art Library
International

89: Peter Stuyvesant chastises Willem Wickendam for
preaching a Baptist sermon
(litho), American School/Pri-
vate Collection/Peter Newark
Pictures/The Bridgeman Art
Library International

95: Library of Congress, Prints
and Photographs Division,
LC-USZC4-12217

98: AP Photo/ Beth J. Harpaz

Index